THE WAY BACK TO
MAYBERRY

THE WAY BACK TO
MAYBERRY

LESSONS
FROM
A SIMPLER
TIME

• JOEY FANN •

BROADMAN
&HOLMAN
PUBLISHERS

Nashville, Tennessee

0-8054-2420-2

Published by Broadman & Holman Publishers,
Nashville, Tennessee

Dewey Decimal Classification: 241
Subject Heading: CHRISTIAN LIFE / ANDY GRIFFITH
SHOW

Library of Congress Card Catalog Number: 00-058491

All photos courtesy of *The Andy Griffith Show* Rerun Watchers
Club (TAGSRWC).

Unless otherwise stated all Scripture citation is from the NIV,
the Holy Bible, New International Version, copyright © 1973,
1978, 1984 by International Bible Society. Other versions cited
are the NKJV, the New King James Version, copyright © 1979,
1980, 1982, Thomas Nelson, Inc., Publishers.

Library of Congress Cataloging-in-Publication Data
Fann, Joey, 1965–
    The way back to Mayberry : lessons from simpler times /
Joey Fann.
        p.   cm.
    ISBN 0-8054-2420-2
        1. Christian life. 2. Andy Griffith show (Television pro-
gram) I. Title.
    BV4501.2 .F288 2001
    241—dc21

                                                00-058491
                                                CIP

5 6 7 8 9 10 05 04 03

Dedicated to the memory of Lewis Daniel Harless

Any ability to write I surely received from him.

ACKNOWLEDGMENTS

I would like to thank the following people who each had a part in the creation of this book:

Brad Grasham for his friendship and for reminding me what the spirit of Mayberry is all about; Lee Segrest for his motivation and encouragement; James Kendrick for asking us to do the class; and the Twickenham Church of Christ for providing the vision and opportunity to implement the Mayberry Bible class concept.

Thanks to Pat Allison for his friendship and mastery of Mayberry trivia; Mark Harless who got me hooked on the show in the first place; Allan Newsome for his work with the WBMUTBB Internet Chapter; Winston and Lisa Harless for their help and contacts with the Nashville crowd; and George Lindsey and Tandy Rice for organizing and providing the foreword to the book.

Thanks to my editor Vicki Crumpton for her gentle prompting to write the book; Kenny Holcomb for the cover design; Janis Whipple for making sure it all came together; and Kim Overcash for keeping the paperwork straight.

Special thanks to Mike Milom for his guidance, friendship, and ability to read the fine print; and to Jim Clark for his encouragement, advice, photos for the book, help with the text, and all the work and effort he performs as Presiding Goober of *The Andy Griffith Show* Rerun Watchers Club (TAGSRWC).

And most of all to my wife, Nicole, for her patience, love, insight, and support from the very beginning.

TABLE OF
CONTENTS

THE WAY BACK TO
MAYBERRY

FOREWORD

Hey! It has now been more than forty years since America and eventually much of the world were introduced to *The Andy Griffith Show*. I feel fortunate to have been part of the talented group of people who worked on this beloved TV show. The wonderful characters and stories and the ideal of Mayberry itself are now a revered part of America's entertainment history.

And entertaining indeed was our very simple goal. As Andy Griffith and others of us who were part of Mayberry have observed many times over the years, our mission was simply to do our part in creating the best possible half-hour of television that we could each week.

The stories were gentle, wholesome, and often nostalgic; but above all, they were interesting. Yet, while we knew we were doing good work, few of us, if any, envisioned that decades later audiences would be watching those same episodes in reruns with at least as much enthusiasm as viewers did when we became the top-rated TV show in prime time in the 1960s.

Especially during the last two decades, much has been recorded and written about *The Andy Griffith Show*—including numerous televised documentaries and reunions and about two dozen books. Entire college courses have been devoted to the "Griffith" show. More recently, Bible study groups using Mayberry have begun. This book, of course, is inspired by study materials created and originally used by Joey Fann in one such Bible study at his church.

That thoughtful viewers are able to find meaningful lessons about morality, relationships, and responsibility from

watching *The Andy Griffith Show* is not surprising. After all, Mayberry is a wholesome place where a keen respect for others is depicted in many ways. By the same token, the appeal of good storytelling usually is built upon having the audience become aware of the consequences caused by the characters' actions. That rule of thumb applies whether the story is being told in Mayberry, Shakespeare, or the Bible.

I think it's a fine thing that people are able to find useful inspiration and lessons for life through watching and discussing *The Andy Griffith Show*. This book undoubtedly will be a tool for many people to do just that. But remember this: while you're learning, be sure and don't forget to laugh when Goober "takes off" on Edward G. Robinson and Cary Grant. "Judy, Judy, Judy!"

George Lindsey

INTRODUCTION

I remember really getting into *The Andy Griffith Show* when I was a senior at David Lipscomb University in Nashville, Tennessee. After a hard day of studying and attending classes, my cousin would come over to my apartment with a tape full of old episodes. Mark and I would stay up until all hours of the night watching and having the time of our lives. I know I should have been studying, but watching those shows was fun; it was relaxing; and in a way it was like going home again. No matter how many times we had seen a particular episode, we never got tired of it. Those old shows just seemed to get better and better.

Looking back on that experience, I've often wondered what initially sparked my interest in the show. Sure it was incredibly funny. The interaction between the characters of Mayberry will never be duplicated. It was fun to watch Barney get himself in trouble and then see how Andy would bail him out at the last minute. We laughed with the lovable Gomer Pyle and even had a place in our heart for Otis Campbell, the town drunk. But the more I watched, the more I realized that something else was drawing me to the show. There were lessons to be gathered from Mayberry— real lessons about how ordinary people deal with everyday life.

I began to appreciate the challenges Andy faced raising his son alone. I could identify with Opie as he experienced the excitement and adventures of a young boy growing up. I also saw myself in the character of Barney Fife more than

I would like to admit. It seemed that Barney was always getting into trouble because he was so busy focusing on himself—something I could readily understand. These and many other situations were very familiar to me. They are familiar to us all; yet there was something more. Looking further, I noticed a deeper meaning, one with a spiritual application.

I've often heard preachers tell stories that are familiar to their audience, then transition into a point to be made from Scripture. Given this concept, I thought that using specific situations in *The Andy Griffith Show* to illustrate a point or thought would be a great idea. In the summer of 1998, Brad Grasham and I set out to develop an informal Bible class with *The Andy Griffith Show* as the theme. The purpose was to introduce situations to which people could connect using episodes of *The Andy Griffith Show,* and then take it one step further by reflecting on how God can be at work in those familiar situations in our lives today. The Finding the Way Back to Mayberry class was a great success, and the material has been used by churches and other organizations throughout the country.

When looking back on the lessons from Mayberry, I'm often reminded of experiences and stories from my own life—not that I grew up in Mayberry, but my hometown was pretty similar. In this book, I've selected thirty episodes of *The Andy Griffith Show* that are dear to my heart. Each chapter contains a story line summary of a specific episode followed by my personal reflection of a message presented by the show. I have also included a Scripture, which I hope will give a deeper meaning to the lesson at hand. It is my hope that these pages will take you back to a place where the pace

of life was a little bit slower and to a time where doing the right thing was not the exception, but the rule.

So what are we waiting for? Let's join Barney at the courthouse for a cup of coffee or relax on the front porch with Andy while he plays the guitar. Why, we could even go fishing with Opie as we begin our search for *The Way Back to Mayberry*.

CHAPTER 1

YOU NEVER ASKED

"Opie's Charity"

"Do not judge, or you too will be judged. For in the same way you judge others, you will be judged, and with the measure you use, it will be measured to you. Why do you look at the speck of sawdust in your brother's eye and pay no attention to the plank in your own eye? How can you say to your brother, 'Let me take the speck out of your eye,' when all the time there is a plank in your own eye? You hypocrite, first take the plank out of your own eye, and then you will see clearly to remove the speck from your brother's eye."

Matthew 7:1–5

"Opie's Charity" is an early episode in the series and one that really highlights the incredible acting ability of young Ronny Howard. The interaction between Andy and Opie is classic, and we can see the stage being set for a wonderful father-son relationship that will last for years in our hearts and in reruns. The episode begins with Andy and Opie playing catch. While they are playing, Annabelle Silby comes by to solicit help with the annual children's charity drive she heads up every year. Andy and Annabelle go into the courthouse to discuss the status of the charity drive. While at the courthouse, Annabelle compliments the town's children on their willingness to help out with such a worthy cause. Andy, taking this opportunity to brag, suggests that Opie is probably one of the biggest contributors in his class. However, Annabelle relates that Opie only contributed three cents to the charity drive. The next lowest contributor was five cents, and that was from Roy Pruitt, one of the underprivileged children. Andy is beside himself. He can't believe his son would contribute such a measly amount to a worthy cause like the children's charity drive. When Opie returns to the courthouse, Andy greets him with names like "Moneybags" and "Diamond Jim." Andy proceeds to have a sit-down discussion with his son to discuss the importance of giving. Opie claims he is saving his money to buy his girlfriend, Charlotte, a present. Try as he might, Andy just can't get the point across to his son that he should give more to the charity drive.

That night at supper, Andy still cannot convince Opie that it is important for him to be generous in his giving. Finally, Andy has had it and he sends Opie to his room. While Andy is muttering to himself about how embarrassing it is for the son of the town sheriff to give the least amount to the charity drive, Aunt Bee interjects. Aunt Bee asks Andy to stop and think about what he is saying. Is he more concerned about what other people think than he is about his own son? Is he really ready to give up on his son because of this one incident? Andy realizes what he has done and calls

Opie downstairs. He tells Opie that it is OK to spend all his money on his girlfriend, and it doesn't matter if he buys her a toy or takes her to the movie for two dollars' worth of popcorn. Then Opie says something Andy never expected, something Andy never even considered. "I was saving to buy her a coat," Opie replies. The silence is deafening. "A coat?" Opie continues, "Yeah, the one she's got is kinda worn out." Andy's mouth drops. "But Opie, you never told me what the money was for." Opie's response, "You never asked."

Have you ever considered how easy it is to prejudge someone? To make an assumption before we get all the facts? To automatically assume we know the situation? This episode reminds me of a particular Sunday morning in church. My wife, Nicole, and I were sitting near the front, and two women we didn't know were sitting in front of us. During the service I noticed that the women were whispering to each other. It really didn't bother me at first, but it was a little distracting. As the service went on, the women kept whispering. Now this might be expected behavior from two young children, but these were grown-ups. Everyone knows that you're not supposed to talk in church, especially if you are sitting near the front! The more it went on, the more upset I became, and I eventually lost track of the sermon. I had no idea what the preacher was saying. I just couldn't believe these two women had the nerve to be so distracting in church. How juvenile. How rude.

In a little while the sermon was over and it was time for announcements. One of the announcements was a welcome to the wife of one of our missionaries. She was in the States for a short time and wanted to visit our congregation since we were helping to support their mission effort. She was traveling with a friend, and they were sitting in the front. *What?* I thought. *These two women? The women who have distracted me throughout the entire service? The two that caused me not to get anything from this morning's message? And one of them is the wife of a preacher? You've got to be kidding!*

"By the way," the announcer continued, "our guest doesn't speak English, so when you introduce yourself, her friend will be happy to interpret for you."

There it was. She couldn't understand English. Her friend was her interpreter. That's why they were whispering. Now it all made sense. Suddenly, upon reflection, they didn't seem so distracting. In fact, they were being very discreet trying not to disturb anyone. She just wanted to know what was being said; and her friend was just trying to help. I felt very small. I slowly realized that the reason I was mad and the reason I didn't get anything from the service was not these ladies' fault. It was all my fault because I assumed I knew the situation. I assumed I knew all the facts.

I didn't know the facts. I judged the scene based on my perception—just like Andy did with Opie. He was willing to ignore all the good he knew about his son, and for what? Because he assumed the worst. He assumed his son had done wrong, and he was worried that Opie would embarrass him. How easy it can be to lose our faith in others all because we jump to conclusions, because we prejudge.

That Sunday morning I kept thinking to myself, *You never told me she didn't speak English.* But then again, I never asked.

CHAPTER 2

ANOTHER WORLD

"Man in a Hurry"

My brethren, count it all joy when you fall into various trials, knowing that the testing of your faith produces patience. But let patience have its perfect work, that you may be perfect and complete, lacking nothing.

James 1:2–4, NKJV

Malcolm Tucker is a wealthy businessman from Charlotte. One Sunday he happens to have car trouble a couple of miles outside of Mayberry. Malcolm walks the rest of the way to town and meets Andy coming out of Sunday morning worship. Andy offers to assist Malcolm but warns that it is nearly impossible to get anything done on a Sunday in Mayberry. Malcolm begins to lose patience when Wally, the filling station owner, refuses to fix his car because it is his policy not to work on Sunday. Furthermore, Malcolm is dumbfounded when he learns that he can't even use the telephone because the elderly Mindlebright sisters use the party line to visit on Sunday afternoons, since they are unable to get around very well. Back at the Taylor house, things don't get much better for Malcolm. He explodes into a tirade, screaming that the citizens of Mayberry are living in another world—that this is the twentieth century, and while the whole world is living in a desperate space age, the town of Mayberry shuts down because two old ladies' feet fall asleep.

Out on the front porch Malcolm actually begins to relax as Barney and Andy sing the old spiritual "Church in the Wildwood." But this calm moment is short-lived when Gomer informs Malcolm that his cousin Goober has offered to fix the car. Later, when Gomer returns with the car, Malcolm is surprised that there is no charge for the repair since it was just a clogged fuel line. Goober actually considered it an honor to work on such a fine machine. As Mr. Tucker prepares to leave, he stops and contemplates the events of the afternoon as well as his return to the activities of his hectic life. Malcolm realizes that the very characteristics of Mayberry life that initially frustrated him so much are, in fact, the priorities he needs to establish in his own life. He decides to put his business on hold and stay the night in Mayberry.

I think the reason the episode "Man in a Hurry" is so popular is that we can all see ourselves in Malcolm Tucker. We can all get caught up in our daily activities to the extent that we are blinded to everything else going on around us, and when things don't go our way, we explode! It's a lesson of patience and one I need to remind myself of daily. I expect things to happen on my time. I expect to be in a certain position in life by a certain age, and if I don't make that goal, I become exasperated. One of my struggles is living my life on God's time; and even though I may think that I am ready for the next step, God's plan might be quite different.

I can also understand Malcolm's frustration because I tend to be a very organized person. I start my day with a list

of activities, and I carefully plan my time so as to get everything accomplished. When something happens to disrupt my schedule (and something always does), I get all bent out of shape! Now I'm not saying that order and planning are bad things, but I think they can be taken to the extreme. If I am so regimented that one unexpected event throws me into turmoil, then I might need to reexamine my priorities.

I have often heard the suggestion that every once in a while you should stop and imagine what you would say about yourself if you could attend your own funeral. I'm not talking about reflecting on your lifetime accomplishments, but about the type of person you were. In my case, I don't think I would be proud of how uptight I tended to be; I wouldn't brag about how intolerant I was when I didn't get my own way; and I doubt I would fondly remember how I tended to lose my temper when events in my life didn't go the way I planned. However, by reflecting on my life now, I still have time to make some important changes and to address some things in my life that I can improve. But, like Malcolm, I have to want to make those changes in my life.

Similarly, Malcolm's unplanned visit to Mayberry caused him to consider his own priorities. He was forced to deal with people and situations that were not part of his itinerary. For one day he was not in control; Mayberry was. His initial reaction was to reject everything Mayberry had to offer. He refused to eat Sunday dinner with the Taylors, he refused to relax on the front porch, and he resisted adopting the pace of a Mayberry Sunday afternoon. Malcolm had an attitude we all have at one time or another. He couldn't see past his own busy self. By being blind to everything but ourselves, we, like Malcolm, miss out on so much in life. I believe that when we all look back on our lives, we will wish that our priorities had been a little bit different. We will wish we had spent more time doing the things that really made a difference instead of worrying about the aspects of our lives that didn't mean that much at all. If a visit to Mayberry could adjust Malcolm's priorities in life, maybe we all could stand to have car trouble there every once in a while.

One of my favorite characters in the Bible is Joseph, son of Jacob. In my opinion, Joseph is the example of how to maintain patience and the proper perspective on life. From an early age, injustice and hard times seemed to follow Joseph. He was sold into slavery by his own brothers and was later falsely accused by Potipher's wife. I don't know if I would have been patient enough to wait on God. I think that I would have felt pretty sorry for myself, wondering why all these bad things had happened to me when I hadn't done anything wrong. Joseph, however, was not caught up with his own life. He knew that God was with him and that God had a plan for him. He also had the wisdom to know that God was going to act in His own time. In the end, Joseph's patience paid off. He was placed second in command over all of Egypt and was reunited with his family. So, whenever I feel dejected or angry that the events of my life are not happening in accordance with my plan, remembering Joseph seems to put my life into perspective.

YOU'VE GOT A FRIEND

"Andy on Trial"

"Greater love has no one than this, that he lay down his life for his friends."

John 15:13

The first time I watched "Andy on Trial," I really didn't like it that much. I thought it was a good episode, but it was too serious. For an episode of *The Andy Griffith Show* to be too serious, something must be up! The episode begins with Andy in a big city at the office of Mr. J. Howard Jackson. Mr. Jackson runs a publishing company and produces several newspapers. Andy has come to arrest Mr. Jackson because he failed to appear in court for a traffic violation he received while traveling through Mayberry. It seems Andy had given Mr. Jackson a break and allowed him to continue on his way with the promise that he would return to court. Andy brings Mr. Jackson back to Mayberry and fines him fifteen dollars. Mr. Jackson is outraged. He can't believe that Andy would drag him all the way to the "hick" town of Mayberry for a paltry fifteen dollars. He storms out of the courthouse vowing revenge on Andy.

Unbeknownst to Andy and Barney, Mr. Jackson sends a pretty, young female reporter to Mayberry to gather dirt on Andy—anything he can use against the sheriff. The reporter poses as a college kid on assignment to research small-town governments. Of course, Barney is smitten with the young reporter and offers to show her around Mayberry. During the course of the tour, Barney and the reporter have a soda together at the local diner. Being very discreet, the reporter taps Barney for anything that could be used against Andy. Barney, caught up in all the attention, proceeds to tell the reporter that if he were in charge he would run the sheriff's department differently. Barney continues to complain about crimes going unpunished (Emma Watson's jaywalking) and the blatant unofficial use of the squad car (delivering groceries to a shut-in). As you can imagine, Mr. Jackson uses Barney's words to write a scathing article about Andy's administration.

The episode concludes with a hearing to determine if the charges against Andy can be substantiated. If the charges are true, then Andy will lose his job. The court scene takes a twist when Barney is called to be the star witness against Andy (after all, it was Barney who originated the claims against Andy). Barney reluctantly tells the court that he did say the things printed in the article; however, he never intended his words to be used against Andy. Barney goes on to defend Andy as the best friend he and the town of Mayberry ever had. As to the way Andy runs the sheriff's department, Barney explains that he has yet to master what Andy has been trying to teach him for years, "that when you're dealing with people, you do a whole lot better if you go not so much by the book, but by the heart."

As I stated earlier, I really didn't like this episode the first time I saw it, but since then it has become one of my favorites. Granted, it is more somber than some of the other episodes, but it deals with a very serious issue—the importance of our friends and how easy it is to put our friendships at risk. Stop and think for just a minute about your friends. I'm not talking about acquaintances or even people you may see on a daily basis. I'm talking about the friends you could call any time of the day or night, and you know they would listen—the friends who would defend you under any circumstances, the friends who would never leave your side as long as you needed them to be there. When I think about the people I can count on to be there for me, I feel very blessed because I've leaned on those friends in difficult situations. I can't imagine what I would have done if they hadn't been there to help.

A couple of years ago I was really distraught about a job decision. My current job was not working out as I had planned, and I had an opportunity to go to another company. The decision, however, was not quite that easy. Even though I was unhappy with my current job, I was working for an established company and I knew my job was stable. While the new company had an attractive position and benefits package, it was with a much smaller company and the risks were higher. I had to make a decision and I honestly did not know what to do. That afternoon I called my friend Lincoln. I didn't tell him what was wrong; I just told him I needed to talk. Without questioning the situation, he immediately agreed to meet me at the church. Once there, he suggested we go for a ride, and he drove me around while I spilled my heart about the decision I had to make. Lincoln did a lot of listening; and he offered his advice when I asked; but the point is, he was there for me. I knew he couldn't make my decision for me, but it meant so much that he would just listen and care. When we got back to the church, we prayed about the decision and that I would have the wisdom to do the right thing. After our time together, I felt confident to make the right decision and to make it without looking back. Two years later, I know I made the right decision, and in some way, I owe that to Lincoln. He was there for me and he helped me through a tough time. He was my friend.

However, as much as we depend on friends, how often do we take them for granted? And worse, how often do we damage our friendships by trying to lift ourselves up at their expense? A selfish attitude can go a long way in destroying a friendship. Sometimes we may not even be aware of what we are doing.

In this episode, I'm sure Barney didn't intend to hurt Andy. He was caught up in the moment and was trying to impress the reporter. The last thing on his mind was that what he was saying could hurt his friendship with Andy, but it did. And it can happen to us. Even though we have no malice or ill intentions, we can hurt the very ones we depend on by trying to lift ourselves up. Instead of focusing on ourselves, we should try to incorporate the instruction in the Book of James and humble ourselves so that the Lord will lift us up.

As much as they mean to us, our friends are human and they can fail us just as Barney failed Andy. It helps me to remember that I do have a friend who will not fail me. A friend who has loved me since before I was born. A friend who cared so much for me that He actually died in my stead. A friend who wishes nothing more than to have a close, personal relationship with me. I have to admit that I don't always automatically think of Jesus when I think of my close friends, but I should. He has done so much for me, and even though I often fail Him, He never stops loving me. And when you think about it, isn't that what friendship is all about?

CHAPTER 4

KEEPING THE FAITH

"Andy Forecloses"

"I tell you the truth, if you have faith as small as a mustard seed, you can say to this mountain, 'Move from here to there' and it will move. Nothing will be impossible for you."

Matthew 17:20

In the episode "Andy Forecloses" hard times have befallen Lester Scobey and his family. Unfortunately, Lester has recently lost his job and the family is having a hard time coming up with the rent payment. Lester, his wife, Helen, and their young daughter, Mary, rent a house from department store owner Ben Weaver. And Ben, who is not one to show much compassion, is getting impatient. He even orders Andy to serve an eviction notice on the struggling family. Andy immediately visits the Scobey family to find out what can be done. Lester tells Andy that he is looking for work, but no one seems to be hiring. In the meantime, Helen is pitching in by taking in some extra laundry, but they just can't seem to make ends meet. Andy tells Lester not to worry, and he doesn't mention the eviction notice. He returns to the office with a plan to help the Scobeys. Working together, Andy and Barney quietly raise the needed money to pay off the month's rent of $52.50. However, when Andy presents the money to Ben, he finds that the Scobeys' troubles are just beginning.

When Andy offers the rent money, Ben refuses to take it. Furthermore, Ben points out an obscure clause in the Scobeys' contract, which states that if a payment is missed for any reason, the entire balance of the rent is due. Therefore, instead of $52.50, the Scobeys now owe Ben a whopping $780. Ben makes it clear that if the Scobeys can't come up with the money, they are to be evicted—immediately! Andy knows that Lester and Helen don't have that kind of money, but he refuses to give up. He is determined to find a solution to this problem, no matter what.

Fortunately, Andy's optimism and helpful attitude are contagious. He and Barney organize a town-wide rummage sale to raise money for the Scobeys, and all of Mayberry turns out in support of this worthy cause—that is, everybody but Ben Weaver. Ben is still insistent that Andy serve the foreclosure notice. Andy continues to put Ben off and even tries a few legal maneuvers of his own to avoid serving the notice, but he knows that time is running out. The more Ben pushes, the more Andy wonders if Ben really knows how heartless his actions are. Andy knows that Ben is a shrewd businessman, but he can't believe that Ben would actually put a family out on the street. Andy gambles and decides to use a little reverse psychology.

To Ben's surprise, Andy now says that the time has come for the Scobeys to leave the house. No more time, no more

chances, no more feeling sorry for them. Ben enthusiastically agrees, and they proceed to the Scobeys' residence. When they get there, Andy is very gruff with Lester, insisting that he and his family leave now. Lester attempts to get a few things together, but Andy refuses to give him any more time. At this point Lester and Helen are at a complete loss about what to do. They can't pay the rent and they have nowhere to go. Slowly Ben begins to see what is really happening. The house is no longer just a structure on a valuable piece of property where he would eventually like to build a warehouse. It is a home; a home that houses a family in need. Andy continues to badger the Scobeys to the point that Helen breaks down in tears. At this instant, Ben puts a stop to the eviction and tells the Scobeys they can stay. He even offers Lester a job at his department store. As Andy and Ben are leaving, Andy gives Lester and Helen a knowing wink. Lester and Helen realize that Andy was just looking out for them all along. Lester smiles and thanks Andy for all his help. Because of Andy, Lester has a new job and his home is saved. What was once a hopeless situation is now a dream come true.

During the whole ordeal, Andy was the only one that kept a positive attitude. From the first time he went to visit the Scobeys, he was thinking of ways to solve their problem. When the problem suddenly became much worse, he didn't throw up his hands and quit; he just tried that much harder. And when there seemed to be no way out, he made a way out. He refused to be beaten; he refused to quit.

This episode shows that difficult and challenging times will come in life. But what is more important? The challenges we face, or how we face them? When I reflected on this episode, it made me think of a challenge that was handed our family a few years ago. Cancer is something that is supposed to happen to someone else. We get very uneasy talking about it, so we usually don't and just hope that it won't happen to us or to our loved ones. That all changed for my family in 1992. My dad was always healthy. Growing up, I can't remember a single time when he had to miss work, or anything else, due to illness. Even after he had his wisdom teeth taken out later in life, he was up and moving around when people half his age would still be in bed. He was the last person anyone would think would ever get sick. But he did.

My dad was diagnosed with colon cancer, and the initial prospects were not good. The tumor was too large to operate on, so radiation and chemotherapy treatments were the only course of action. As you can imagine, this situation had a profound affect on our family. It caused us to realize how quickly our lives can change and that we are not guaranteed good health forever. However, this particular situation made me realize something else. When something bad happens to you, you have a choice. You can react with hopelessness and bitterness and feel sorry for yourself; or you can make the best of it, try to learn from it, and maybe even use your experience to help others.

My dad did not panic. Neither did he fall into a state of deep depression or give up. He approached the situation with as much optimism as possible. During the initial treatments, I never heard him complain or gripe about how unfair his situation was. He always had a good attitude and went on with his life the best he could. At the end of the treatments, he did receive some good news. The tumor had shrunk, and the doctors were confident that they could go in and operate with some degree of success. I remember the feeling of helplessness while waiting during the operation, which took much longer than the doctors originally antici-pated. There were some complications and he would spend several months recovering, but the surgery was considered successful. I still remember spending time with my dad a few days after that initial surgery. Even after all he had been through and knowing that he would face many more months of recovery, you would never know that anything was wrong. His mood and outlook on life were the same. He refused to let this life-threatening situation get him down.

It has been more than seven years since my dad was di-agnosed with cancer. His oncologist recently told him that he doesn't need to see my dad again because the chances of the cancer's return are so low. We are all thankful for his re-covery, and I know this situation has given us a greater ap-preciation of the time we do have together. But this situation also taught me something else. I've learned that bad things will happen to us in this life, but the issue is not the tragedy itself; it's how we respond. To some extent, we do have a choice. We can choose to get bitter or to get better. My dad is a great example of how to get better.

CHAPTER 5
FIXING OUR EYES

"Rafe Hollister Sings"

But the LORD said to Samuel, "Do not consider his appearance or his height, for I have rejected him. The LORD does not look at the things man looks at. Man looks at the outward appearance, but the LORD looks at the heart."

1 Samuel 16:7

"Rafe Hollister Sings" opens with Barney trying out for the annual Mayberry Musicale. However, Barney's musical talent isn't quite up to the level Barney thinks it is. In fact, when farmer Rafe Hollister enters the courthouse and finds out that the noise he hears is coming from Barney, Rafe asks Andy how long the deputy has been ailing! Rafe is a country fella who has been busted for moonshinin' a time or two in Mayberry. But even with his checkered past, Rafe's heart is as good as gold. Rafe takes an interest in Barney's upcoming tryout and agrees to sing along with Barney as Andy accompanies on the guitar. It soon becomes obvious that Rafe has a beautiful voice. Andy encourages Rafe to try out for the Musicale, but Rafe is hesitant. Barney thinks that Rafe shouldn't try out because only people with proper training should take part in such events. Barney tells Rafe to keep singing in the bathtub but not to try out because Rafe might embarrass himself. In a hilarious scene, Barney asks Rafe what he would do if he were asked to sing a cappella at the tryouts. Rafe admits that he wouldn't know what to do. When Andy asks Barney what he would do if he were asked to sing a cappella, Barney unknowingly shows his ignorance by singing the words "a cappella" to the tune of "La Cucaracha."

Rafe decides to try out for the musicale, and he wins. Musicale director, John Masters, expresses his approval and appreciation of Rafe's talent to Andy in the courthouse. Unfortunately, not everyone is pleased that Rafe won. The head of the Mayberry chapter of the ladies league, Mrs. Jeffries, and Mayor Stoner do not think that Rafe Hollister is an appropriate choice for a high-class event such as the Musicale. They inform Andy that Rafe must not be the representative from Mayberry. Andy disagrees with the mayor and Mrs. Jeffries but does agree to go see Rafe. However, when he finds out how much winning the contest means to Rafe and his family, Andy decides that he cannot let Rafe down.

Andy returns to the mayor with the news that he has not told Rafe he can't sing. Andy tries to appease the mayor by saying that he will work on Rafe's appearance so that he will be presentable at the Musicale. The mayor reluctantly agrees but says he will hold Andy personally responsible for Rafe's appearance. Andy does what he can and actually ends up giving Rafe a new suit of clothes. Andy tells Rafe that the suit has been issued from the state as part of a rehabilitation program from Rafe's previous arrest. Rafe agrees to wear the suit, but it obviously makes him uncomfortable. When the mayor and Mrs. Jeffries see Rafe in the suit, they agree that it will do, but they tell Andy to be sure that Rafe does not associate with anyone.

Now the truth is out. The concern about Rafe's appearance was just a front to cover their true feelings. The mayor and Mrs. Jeffries do not consider Rafe to be worthy of their association. At this point, Andy knows what he must do. It is time to forget about the mayor and Mrs. Jeffries and stand up for what he knows is right. Andy and Rafe perform at the Musicale, and Rafe does a wonderful job, drawing the applause of the town. But Rafe isn't dressed in his suit; he is dressed as Rafe Hollister normally dresses—in his boots and overalls!

Looking back on this story, it is easy to notice the issue of prejudice. Even though we don't condone it, we can understand why the mayor and some of the other Mayberry socialites were against Rafe Hollister singing at the musicale. We can understand it because we've seen it ourselves; perhaps we have even been guilty of such behavior. I often wonder what I would do if someone dressed as Rafe Hollister came into my office or visited my church one Sunday morning. Would I welcome him as an honored guest, or would I ignore him and hope he would go away? I would like to think I would treat him well, but sometimes I think my behavior would be more like that of the mayor.

This episode also makes me ask the question, What is it really like to be a victim of prejudice? Sure, I have been shunned or treated differently because of certain external factors on occasion, but I don't believe I have ever experienced true prejudice. I couldn't imagine a lonelier feeling than to be in a situation where I was different from everyone else until it actually happened to me.

A few years ago I was fortunate enough to visit the city of Cairo, Egypt, on a weeklong business trip. I was traveling with my manager, and the purpose of our trip was to demonstrate our company's software capability to members of the Egyptian military. After a long flight, we finally arrived in Cairo. When you get off the plane in Egypt, you immediately become aware that you are not in the United States. The first thing I noticed was the heat. If the airport had air-conditioning, it wasn't working that day. Furthermore, when you rent a car in Cairo, you also rent the driver. That didn't make sense to me until we actually got into traffic. Traffic lights do exist in the city, but I'm not sure why because nobody pays attention to them. Basically, you just try to maneuver through the intersections without hitting the other cars, herd of goats, or whatever else might be in the road.

When we got to the hotel, I noticed that armed guards were stationed outside. I later found out that the hotel was hosting an international conference of some sort, and the security was high. These weren't security guards, but actual Egyptian soldiers with actual Egyptian machine guns. I guess the fact that the hotel was so well guarded should have made me feel better, but it didn't. I slowly realized that the home I knew, a small patch in northern Alabama, was literally a world away.

For most of the week, I worked at a small subcontractor shop installing software and configuring computer systems in preparation for the demonstrations we would give toward the end of the week. Luckily, some of the businessmen there spoke a little English, so it was fairly easy to communicate. My travel companion, Jim, was also there to sort out the logistics of the upcoming demonstrations. Our primary presentation was to be made at the Egyptian War College, which was located at a military base near the city. As you can imagine, the security on the base was very tight, especially for a foreign national. The first day we arrived at the facility, I was forced to wait at a guard shack outside the main gate for about an hour while they processed the paperwork. Needless to say, the guard shack was not air-conditioned, and the facilities were pretty sparse. However, after we finally got into the complex, the surroundings improved drastically. The building to which we were assigned was very plush, with a hint of royalty. The hallways were very formal and decorated with a variety of flags, plaques, and other displays of military power.

We were taken to a fairly large auditorium to set up our computer equipment. The demonstration was to be held the next day, so I immediately got to work. I quickly became immersed in setting up the computers and lost all track of time. At one point Jim told me he would have to return to the hotel to meet with another representative. I acknowledged his comment, but I didn't stop what I was doing. I vaguely remember assuming that I would ride back with one of the Egyptian subcontractors who had originally brought us to the base. About an hour later, I began to finish up what I was doing and slowly realized that I was alone and had been for some time. For the first time, I realized that when Jim said he was going back to the hotel that meant everyone in our party was going back to the hotel, except me.

It was at that point that I felt totally alone. I was in the middle of the Egyptian War College by myself—one English-speaking, white American in the middle of several hundred soldiers, colonels, and generals of a foreign army. The guards at the door didn't give me the time of day. No one coming in or going out would even acknowledge me. I remember thinking that I might never get out of this place. What if they think I'm a spy and throw me in some Egyptian prison for the rest of my life? Although we share the same first name, I really didn't want to end up like the Old Testament Joseph who was thrown into an Egyptian prison even though he was innocent.

It is hard to describe that feeling of loneliness until you experience it yourself. You're around a lot of people, but no one knows you. You need their help, but they aren't interested in helping. You search the crowd for a friendly face, but there is none to be found. I felt totally alone. I quietly finished what I was doing, then sat down to wait. What was I going to do? Who would I call, like I could figure out the Egyptian phone system anyway. Suddenly I saw a familiar face. Yes, it was one of the guys from the office, one of the subcontractors. He came up to me with a big smile and said, "Joe!" That was the only English he spoke, but I didn't care. He knew me. He was there to help me. I honestly don't believe I have ever been happier to see someone than I was at that moment. I was quite relieved that I hadn't been forgotten and I was not going to spend the night in the stockade.

We left the complex and I rode back to the hotel in the banged-up car of my new best friend, Ahmed Salah. All the way back to the hotel, he described the sites and scenery of his city in great detail. Of course, I couldn't understand a word he said, but I didn't care. I was with a friend, and he was taking me back home—even if it was just to the hotel. A victim of prejudice? Hardly, but I could feel the loneliness of being in a crowd without a friend and having no one to turn to. I felt completely helpless. But out of the crowd came a familiar face, someone who cared about me, and what a difference that made.

Back to the episode, it is easy to see the meanness of the mayor and Mrs. Jeffries, but I would suggest that in real life it's harder to see our own insensitivity. It's very easy to make quick decisions based on external factors. It's much harder to get past the external and see the person inside. In His ministry, Jesus made it a practice to get past the external. He could see past the dishonesty of a tax collector. He could see something underneath the temper of an ordinary fisherman. He could see into the heart of the woman at the well. He could find the good in everyday people. He wasn't so caught up with the external factors that sway our attention. He was more concerned with the internal attributes that provide a window into a person's heart.

Because of his appearance and social status, Rafe never had a chance with the mayor and Mrs. Jeffries. Look at what they missed—a warm, funny, and talented individual. It makes you wonder about the relationships we may miss because we are too quick to judge people on external appearances.

CHAPTER 6
FAMILY VALUES

"Opie and the Spoiled Kid"

*Children, obey your parents in the Lord, for this is right.
"Honor your father and mother"—which is the first com-
mandment with a promise—"that it may go well with
you and that you may enjoy long life on the earth."
Fathers, do not exasperate your children; instead, bring
them up in the training and instruction of the Lord.*

Ephesians 6:1–4

In the episode "Opie and the Spoiled Kid" Opie meets a
new kid in town named Arnold Winkler. Opie soon finds
out that Arnold is wise to the ways of the world and pretty
much has life figured out. After all, Arnold has been
around—he used to live in Raleigh! Arnold can't believe all
the chores Opie has to do just to receive a twenty-five-cent
allowance. Arnold tells Opie that his father sure saw him
coming because kids nowadays should get at least seventy-
five cents for their allowance, and without working for it.
In fact, Arnold shows Opie his seventy-dollar bike he received from his dad just because, in Arnold's words, his dad
owed it to him. Opie is now confused. Arnold says that
Opie shouldn't have to work for his allowance, but Opie

has always worked for his allowance. He decides to ask his pa if the rules have really changed.

What follows is one of the more memorable scenes of the show. At the courthouse, Opie has an open and honest discussion with Andy about the rules for kids and parents. Opie tries to explain that all the kids are getting seventy-five cents for allowance these days, and they don't have to work for it. Andy calmly explains that there aren't any set rules for parents and kids and that each parent has the responsibility for determining how to raise his or her own child. Andy continues with how important it is to learn the responsibility of working for a reward. Andy asks Opie if he doesn't feel good after a hard day's work. Opie replies, "Yeah, good and tired." A defeated Opie begins to realize that he will not get an allowance raise, and he will have to continue to work for the twenty-five cents that he currently earns.

After the father and son chat, Arnold tells Opie that he isn't trying hard enough. He needs to fight for his rights by talking back and throwing tantrums. Opie decides to give these new techniques a try. Opie returns to the courthouse to attempt another allowance negotiation. First, Opie tries to hold his breath, but Andy just compliments him on doing a good lung exercise. Next, Opie says that he's crying and can't stop, but again Andy seems unconcerned. As a final resort, Opie falls to the floor kicking and screaming. Andy asks Opie what he is doing, and when Opie replies that he is throwing a tantrum, Andy tells him not to get his clothes dirty. This is not the reaction a dejected Opie had hoped to produce.

Meanwhile, Arnold continues to show his disrespect for any kind of authority by riding his bicycle on the sidewalk, even after Barney gives him a warning. Finally, Arnold flaunts the law one too many times, and Andy confiscates the bike. Arnold is furious and screams at Andy that he is going to go tell his dad. Andy tells Arnold to do just that and to bring his dad by the courthouse. What follows is a scene that shows Arnold's true colors. Arnold wants his bike back, and it doesn't matter what it takes to get it. Arnold even offers his dad to be put in jail if that will get his bike back. At this point, Arnold's dad realizes what a spoiled and disrespectful kid he has raised. At Andy's suggestion, he takes Arnold out back to an old-fashioned woodshed where he gives Arnold a much-needed attitude adjustment.

This scene is also a powerful lesson for Opie. He sees very clearly the results of Arnold's disrespect for his own father. After Arnold's final tirade, just the look on Opie's face speaks volumes. Forget the nice bike and the big allowance. Opie doesn't want to be like Arnold. Opie now understands that Andy was just trying to do what was best for him. He begins to see the value of Andy's guidance. Opie later apologizes by asking Andy if he happens to need anyone to do some chores around the house. Andy forgives his son and compliments Opie on having the courage to admit his fault. Andy even offers to raise Opie's allowance from twenty-five to twenty-seven cents. When asked what he will do with the extra money, Opie replies that he will buy a bell. Andy wonders what his son would want with a bell. Opie responds that some day he will have enough money saved up to put a bike under it. It looks like Andy's guidance and instruction are already starting to pay off.

On Saturday mornings at our local church, we perform an outreach program to help those in our community who

are less fortunate. We provide food, clothing, and other household items for people who might be down on their luck or having a hard time making ends meet for one reason or another. The people show up at the church, and we spend a few minutes with them just to find out what's going on in their lives and to better learn how we might be able to help. It is a very sobering and rewarding experience. These people make you realize how blessed you are and how insignificant your problems seem compared to theirs. It is also a blessing to see some of these people rise from the ashes to make a better life for themselves. Though I don't always look forward to going to church on Saturday mornings to do this work, at the end of the day I'm always glad I went.

One particular Saturday a young mother and her son came in. I sat down with her, and I could tell by looking into her eyes that she was struggling. She told me that her husband worked in construction and had recently been injured. Apparently the injury was serious enough that he hadn't been able to work for several days. He didn't receive workman's compensation, so the family's income had stopped. Although she usually stayed home with her young son, she was in the process of looking for a job.

Her son, Jacob, was probably about two years old. He was old enough to walk, but he wasn't talking much yet. He was an adorable little boy with haunting blue eyes. He was very shy and clung to his mama when I asked him his name. After a few minutes, he warmed up a little bit and began to feel more at home. Being mischievous, as most little boys are, he began to wander around the room. His mother, being conscious of her son, reminded him that they had talked about being good before coming in. That reminded me of many occasions when I was a little boy and my mom would have a talk about being good before we went into a department store or restaurant. Unfortunately, in my case the conversation was soon forgotten. Jacob, however, was obviously a well-behaved little boy and responded to his mother's words by having a seat next to her. Jacob's mother and I continued to talk for a little while longer.

When we talk to each person, we offer to have a prayer with them. Usually we ask if there is anything specific the person would like us to pray for. At first I was uncomfortable praying with people I had just met, but the more I did it, the more I realized how appreciative people are for this simple act. I offered to pray for Jacob and his mom, and she said that would be OK. Then she spoke to Jacob and said, "Do you remember how to pray? Do you remember Grandma praying with you and teaching you how?" Jacob responded by bowing his head, and he sat perfectly still while I prayed for him and his family. After we were through talking, I helped Jacob's mom load the groceries and clothes into their small truck, and as they were driving away, I began to think about what she had said.

I wondered why Jacob hadn't learned to pray from his own mother and father. Did they leave that important training solely up to the grandmother? I wasn't blaming his parents because there was no way I could know all the struggles they were going through. In fact, all I could see in the mother's eyes was a lot of sadness. But somewhere the responsibility of instilling a basic value to her son had been lost. It seems that this generation has lost sight of the responsibility to instill values into its children. We are led to believe that it is the church's responsibility, or the schools', or the government's, or the grandparents'. But what is so important in our lives that would keep us from teaching our children the values that will last a lifetime? The values that define who we are and what we are about? Have we become so distracted that we have lost sight of that very core responsibility?

I'm sure the daily schedule of a small-town sheriff would pale in comparison to our busy schedules today, but there are some things to notice from Andy's example. He was available. Opie could go to his father anytime he wanted, and Andy was never too busy to talk. He was understanding. No matter what the subject, Andy would give Opie a chance to explain himself, and he would listen. He was firm in what was right. Even though Opie was tempted to take the easy way out, Andy gently but firmly guided him in the right direction. Andy knew that this training at an early age would pay off later in life. Andy put it well when he said, "If we don't teach children to live in society today, what's going to happen when they grow up?"

CHAPTER 7

THINGS UNSEEN

"Mr. McBeevee"

Now faith is being sure of what we hope for and certain of what we do not see.

Hebrews 11:1

The episode "Mr. McBeevee" is a wonderful story about faith. The show opens with Opie and Andy "horsing around" with Opie's imaginary horse, Blackie. At breakfast Barney actually believes Opie has a new horse and is embarrassed when he realizes that Blackie is just a product of Opie's imagination. Barney makes it clear to Andy that he isn't so thrilled by Opie's imagination. Later, Opie begins discussing a new friend he met in the woods named Mr. McBeevee. As Opie describes him, Mr. McBeevee walks among the treetops and wears a big, shiny, silver hat. Andy and Barney don't realize that Mr. McBeevee is actually a real telephone line crewman. Andy is happy to go along with the game until Opie shows up with a small hatchet and a quarter, both supposedly given to him by Mr. McBeevee. At this point Andy accompanies Opie to the woods to find this mysterious character, but Mr. McBeevee has already been called away on another assignment.

Based on Opie's incredible description of Mr. McBeevee
and the fact that he is nowhere to be found, Andy concludes
that Opie is lying. Back in Opie's room, Andy tells Opie that
if he will just say that Mr. McBeevee is not real, all will be
forgotten. However, if Opie does not say that Mr. McBeevee
is just make-believe, he will be punished. Though he is

tempted to take the easy way out, Opie stands his ground and insists that Mr. McBeevee is indeed real. At first Andy is disappointed, but upon closer examination of Opie's determination, he tells his son that he believes him. Downstairs Barney can't believe that Andy actually admits he now believes in Mr. McBeevee. Andy corrects Barney by saying that he doesn't believe in Mr. McBeevee, but he does believe in Opie.

This episode reminds me of the true definition of faith. That faith is not based on evidence, and it does not always make sense. Faith is not something we conclude from a logical thought process, because faith is inherently illogical. Opie's description of Mr. McBeevee illustrates this point perfectly. From Opie's description, Andy has no reason to believe that what his son is saying is true. We as humans pride ourselves in our logic, and we believe that everything real must have a logical explanation. Our problems begin when we are called to believe in something that is not supported by evidence we can understand.

If I were to relate myself to one of Jesus' disciples, it would have to be Thomas. Thomas was no doubt a faithful follower and friend of Jesus. But even after accompanying Jesus throughout his ministry, Thomas's faith was still weak. Following the death of Jesus, Thomas boldly stated that he would not believe Jesus had risen unless he could actually feel the scars of His hands and side. Many times I feel my faith to be that of Thomas. I want to see the evidence before I commit. I want to examine the facts, then come to my own conclusion. However, facts are not what faith is all about. We are never guaranteed that we will understand everything in this life. The real fact is that there will probably be more

I don't understand about this life than what little I may be able to comprehend.

In the episode, when Andy was forced to decide whether or not to believe in his son, he had two options. First, he could have based his decision solely on the evidence, including any preconceived opinions he had about his son's active imagination. In that case, he would have concluded that Opie was lying about the existence of Mr. McBeevee. His second option was more difficult. He would have to see past what he understood about the situation and look into the heart of his young son, and regardless of the evidence, believe in his son. That is hard to do, but it is exactly what we are called to do as Christians. To look past all the suffering and injustice in this world—all the things we could point to and say, "If God loves me, then why is this happening to me!?" Instead, we are called to have the faith that even though we don't understand everything, God will do what is right. Andy said it best when he explained why he believed in Opie, "I guess it's a time like this when you're asked to believe something that just don't seem possible; that's the moment that decides whether you've got faith in somebody or not."

Thomas eventually got his wish. He got to feel the scars of Jesus and confirm that He had indeed risen from the dead. But it was the response of Jesus that gives me hope today. Jesus told Thomas, "Because you have seen me, you have believed; blessed are those who have not seen and yet have believed." These words give me the strength and the motivation to keep going until the day when I can feel His scars myself.

CHAPTER 8
ABOVE THE LAW

"Bailey's Bad Boy"

*Submit yourselves for the Lord's sake to every authority
instituted among men: whether to the king, as the
supreme authority, or to governors, who are sent by him
to punish those who do wrong and to commend those who
do right. For it is God's will that by doing good you
should silence the ignorant talk of foolish men. Live as
free men, but do not use your freedom as a cover-up for
evil; live as servants of God.*

1 Peter 2:13–16

Over the past year several people have asked me, "What
does a forty-year-old sitcom have to do with the morals and
values that we as Christians try to incorporate into our lives
today?" I obviously think we can learn several lessons from
Mayberry, or you wouldn't be reading this now! But there are
a few episodes that really make the point, and "Bailey's Bad
Boy" is one of them. This episode begins with a traffic accident. Someone has run a farmer's truck off the road and left
the scene of the crime. When Andy and Barney catch up
with the perpetrator, they find a nineteen-year-old named
Ronald Bailey (played by Bill Bixby). Ron is the son of a

powerful man in the state, and he expects to be treated with respect. Even though Andy has heard of Ron's dad, he remains unimpressed. Andy is more concerned with the fact that Ron left the scene of the accident without even a thought that someone might have been hurt. However, Ron is more concerned about being on his way and asks Andy how much it will cost for everyone to just forget the incident.

Andy explains to Ron that things don't work that way in Mayberry, and Ron is taken to the courthouse. Ron is beside himself. He can't believe he is stuck in some hick town because a hick sheriff is too stupid to take a bribe. To make matters worse, it is the weekend and Ron is unable to reach his father on the phone. He resigns himself to the fact that he just might be stuck in Mayberry for a while.

The next twenty-four hours become very important in Ron's life—because Andy takes an interest in the young man. Instead of just leaving him in jail, Andy takes Ron with him on his weekend activities. Andy, Ron, and Opie go fishing, and Ron begins to have a good time until he suspects that Andy is being nice to him because Andy is really afraid of his powerful father. Andy is disappointed that he is not making progress with the boy, but he doesn't give up.

The next afternoon after Sunday dinner, Andy and Opie are talking on the porch. Opie admits to Andy that he accidentally broke a neighbor's window while playing baseball. Opie asks Andy if he is mad, and Andy says no. Andy then asks Opie not to get mad when he tells him that he will not get an allowance until the window is paid for. Opie contemplates the consequences of his actions, and he accepts Andy's punishment. Later Ron asks Andy why he didn't bail the little fellow out. Andy explains that if he always bails Opie out when he is young, then Opie will come to expect it when he gets older. At this point, Ron begins to see Andy's point.

The next day at the courthouse, Ron's lawyer shows up. When the lawyer is unsuccessful at getting Andy to drop the whole matter, he reverts to plan B. The lawyer brings in Fletch, the farmer Ron originally ran off the road. At the lawyer's prompting, Fletch admits that the accident was his fault, not Ron's. Andy, who is wise to the game, realizes that Fletch has been paid off and begins to let Ron out of the cell. However, instead of leaving with the lawyer, Ron states that the accident was his fault and that he wants to stay and face the consequences. The lawyer asks Ron what he should tell the boy's father. Andy suggests he should tell the father that his son broke a window and now wants to stand on his own two feet.

This issue of personal responsibility reminds me of a specific incident in my early teenage years. When I was in the eighth grade, basketball was the sport to play. I went to a fairly small middle school that didn't have a football or baseball team. This was before soccer was the rage, so that particular sport wouldn't be coming along for a few years. We did have track, but there weren't many track meets and it was no big deal to be on the team. If you wanted to run track, you were, by default, on the team. Basketball was a different story. The basketball team was very competitive, and we played several schools around the region. From an eighth-grade boy's point of view, if you wanted to be cool, popular, and an athlete, you could reach no higher pinnacle than to be on the basketball team.

The boys basketball team at West Middle School was coached by a man named Leroy Jackson. Coach Jackson was a tall, athletic man who commanded respect just by his presence. In addition to his basketball responsibilities, Coach Jackson taught seventh grade physical science. Coach Jackson was a strict disciplinarian, but he also made his classes a lot of fun. He was a very vibrant man, always full of life and energy.

It was with that life and energy that Coach Jackson handled his basketball team. From day one, he made it very clear that a certain level of behavior and responsibility was expected from each team member. The rules would be followed, or consequences would result, no exceptions. In the first two weeks of practice, we never saw a basketball. We spent the entire two hours of practice running or participating in some other conditioning drill. Before the first game of the season, our team had dropped from twenty-five to fifteen players. Looking back on it, I realized that the two weeks of "torture" were just Coach Jackson's way of weeding out the boys who weren't willing to give their all.

As the season progressed, we began to see the discipline and conditioning pay off. We were a relatively small team with limited depth, and we would routinely get taunted and jeered by the opposing team before the game. However, once the game wore on, it was apparent that we were in much better physical condition. We ended up winning games we would surely have lost if it weren't for our practice and conditioning.

As I mentioned, in addition to all the practice and conditioning, Coach Jackson demanded and expected a strict adherence to team rules. I remember one time when I was sent to after-school detention for being disruptive in a class. Even though the detention was only for thirty minutes, I knew I

was in trouble because Coach Jackson expected us to be dressed and on the court fifteen minutes after school was over. Immediately after class, I went to the library where detention was held and sat by myself in the far corner with my back to the door. I was clinging to the hope that Coach Jackson wouldn't miss me for the extra fifteen minutes and that I could slip into the locker room and quickly change clothes without being noticed. At approximately 3:20, I heard a booming voice, "Mr. Fann, is that you in the corner?" Coach Jackson never called us by our first names. It was always Mr. Cole, Mr. Shaw, etc. I slowly turned around and squeaked out a "yes, sir." "Well, Mr. Fann," he boomed, "it seems like you are late for practice." I tried to explain that it wasn't really my fault that I got in trouble, but Coach Jackson would hear none of it. He told me to change and report to him as soon as detention was over.

The next ten minutes were probably the longest of my short life to that point. At 3:30, all of us renegades in detention were released. At that point, all the other kids got to go home. My fate was much worse; I had to go see Coach Jackson. I ran to the locker room and quickly put on my practice uniform. We didn't have a uniform policy at our school, but that didn't stop Coach Jackson from requiring us to wear a very specific practice uniform (down to the kind of socks) every day, no exceptions. After I was dressed, I walked out to the court. The other guys were already practicing. I slowly walked over to Coach Jackson and waited. He didn't yell at me or demand an explanation for my behavior. In fact, he didn't mention the detention at all. He just calmly reminded me that practice started at 3:15 sharp, and that everyone, including me, was expected to be dressed and ready to go. He then asked me if I understood. I told him yes and that it would never happen again. He smiled, patted me on the back, and said that he was glad that we had straightened everything out. I was beginning to feel pretty good until he added that I would spend the remainder of the practice, which was a good hour and a half, running the stairs.

Even for an in-shape eighth-grader, an hour and a half is a long time to run the stairs. At the end of practice, I was completely exhausted, but it made an impression. I messed up and I paid the consequences. I thought about how all the other kids in detention just went home that day. They probably didn't give it another thought, and they would probably be back in detention soon. I was never sent to detention again while at West Middle School. Coach Jackson had made his point, and I remembered.

In the episode, we're not given any information as to who might have been influential in Ron Bailey's life. But it was obvious that no one had taught him about personal responsibility, that is, until he met Andy. When I was growing up, I had several great role models to look up to. Both my grandfathers were good men and had strong spiritual and work ethics. My own father was a man of his word and taught me by his example the importance of personal responsibility. But others outside my family also provided the guidance and example I needed during those impressionable years. Friends, teachers, and coaches helped to instill those values that would become so important later in life. Coach Leroy Jackson was one of those people. Yes, he taught me how to be a good basketball player; but more importantly, he taught me how to be a good person.

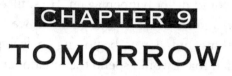

CHAPTER 9

TOMORROW

"Opie's Hobo Friend"

Do everything without complaining or arguing, so that
you may become blameless and pure, children of God
without fault in a crooked and depraved generation, in
which you shine like stars in the universe as you hold out
the word of life—in order that I may boast on the day of
Christ that I did not run or labor for nothing.

Philippians 2:14–16

One reason that the episode "Opie's Hobo Friend" stands out in my mind is that actor Buddy Ebsen plays the hobo. Most of us remember Buddy Ebsen as Jed Clampett on *The Beverly Hillbillies* as well as his starring role in *Barnaby Jones*. In this appearance, Buddy turns in a very believable performance as the hobo who ends up having quite an effect on young Opie. Andy and Opie meet the hobo who identifies himself as David Browne (that's Browne with an 'e') while fishing one day. Later on, Barney runs Mr. Dave in for vagrancy, but Andy doesn't want to needlessly hassle the man. Andy offers Mr. Dave a temporary job trimming the hedges around his house.

The more Opie gets to know Mr. Dave, the more impressed he becomes. You see, Mr. Dave is not like anyone else Opie has ever known. He doesn't have a regular place to live and he doesn't have a job, but to Opie, Mr. Dave seems to be having the time of his life. In one scene Mr. Dave shows Opie that he doesn't need money to get gumballs from the machine; he just needs to know the magic word. "Tuscarora," Mr. Dave shouts, and sure enough, a gumball appears from the machine. What Opie doesn't know is that Mr. Dave has jimmied the machine from the back. Mr. Dave explains that this is not stealing because the machine doesn't want or need the gumball. Therefore it's OK for Opie to have as many gumballs as he wants.

Later at the Taylor house, Mr. Dave and Opie are deciding just how the shrubs should be trimmed. Mr. Dave suggests several approaches, including a formal shape similar to that of Buckingham Palace, or maybe an oriental design, which would include the creation of animal shapes. Opie reminds Mr. Dave that his pa usually just "lops off the tops." During this discussion, Mr. Dave pretends to be interrupted by a fish that just jumped in the lake miles away. Opie is incredulous that Mr. Dave can hear the fish from such a distance, but Mr. Dave explains his talent by telling Opie that he is part Indian. Mr. Dave suggests that they leave the shrubs and go fishing because tomorrow is the perfect day to start any job. Opie begins to believe that the hobo life is the way to go. You can do whatever you want whenever you want, and there are no apparent consequences. This attitude begins to affect Opie as he lets his household chores go and is even picked up by Barney for missing school.

Finally, Andy has enough of this behavior and decides to pay a visit to Mr. Dave down by the train tracks. Andy explains that he is concerned because Opie has begun to imitate Mr. Dave's way of life. Mr. Dave again touts the advantages of his lifestyle and tells Andy that he should let Opie decide what type of life is best for him. Andy reminds Mr. Dave that Opie is just a child and that he will grab at the first shiny thing with ribbons on it. But by the time he finds out that there is a hook, it will be too late. Mr. Dave doesn't argue with Andy and offers to leave town, which in Mr. Dave's mind will solve Andy's problem. Andy reminds Mr. Dave that his problems have just begun. Andy has a lot of unscrambling to do because Opie still thinks that Mr. Dave hung the moon.

Looking back on the story, Mr. Dave has an interesting view of life. He prides himself on living by his wits, and he doesn't care if he has to "bend the law" a little bit now and then to make ends meet. He has developed a lifestyle that suits him just fine and he seems to be very happy. Characteristic of the series, this episode provides many lessons—from Opie's impressionable nature to Andy's struggle to raise his son the best way he knows how. However, I believe Mr. Dave provides us a few lessons as well.

I doubt it was easy being a hobo back in those days. I'm sure Mr. Dave met several "Barneys" who wanted to throw him in jail or run him out of town simply because he didn't fit into the current society. Amid his troubles though, Mr. Dave seems pretty content. Nothing really bothers him too much, and he seems rather proud of himself for living the life that other men only dream of. However, a couple of things about Mr. Dave were all too familiar to me. One is his rationalization. Have you ever noticed how rationalizing a situation gets easier each time you do it? The first time you are faced with doing something you know is wrong, it can

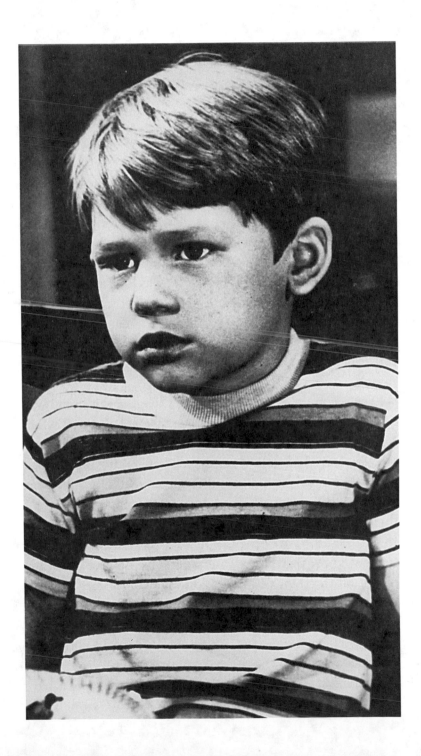

be difficult to rationalize to yourself why it would be OK to go ahead and do it. But the second time you face that same choice, it becomes a little easier. Each subsequent time you are presented with the same situation, it becomes easier and easier to rationalize why you are justified in your decision.

I believe that's what happened to Mr. Dave. Obviously Mr. Dave knew that breaking the law was wrong. But think about the scene at the gumball machine. He had rationalized to himself (and to Opie) that stealing was OK. He thought it was fine to break the law now and then as long as it provided him the means to take care of himself. I know that I can be guilty of the same behavior. I may not steal to get out of working for a living, but I can just as easily rationalize my errant behavior as long as my attitude is focused on serving myself.

The second characteristic of Mr. Dave that hit home was his procrastination. Remember the scene at the porch when Mr. Dave states that tomorrow is the perfect day to start any job. Mr. Dave had gotten pretty good at putting off the task at hand, so much so that you didn't even realize what he was doing until he was already gone. In the past, whenever I thought about procrastination, being lazy immediately came to mind. But I don't believe you have to be lazy to procrastinate. I know that in my case several factors can cause me to put off the things I know I should do. For me, fear is a powerful detractor from my productivity—fear of rejection, fear that my abilities won't suffice, fear that no matter how hard I try I won't succeed. These are all very real feelings that can take away from the things I try to accomplish.

In the end, Mr. Dave realizes the negative effect he is having on Opie. He decides to help Andy out by "stealing" an old purse belonging to Aunt Bee, a purse she has recently thrown out in the trash. When Barney brings Mr. Dave in on charges of theft, Opie just can't believe it. Even Opie knows that Aunt Bee's purse is where she keeps the money to buy food for the family. Opie's opinion of Mr. Dave is dashed, and he even gives back the intricate fishing lure that Mr. Dave had given him earlier. The crushed look on Opie's face tells the whole story. He finally sees the true consequences of such a lifestyle. Andy realizes what Mr. Dave has done and is appreciative that he came back to set things straight. However, Mr. Dave is reluctant to take any credit for his actions. He doesn't apologize for his lifestyle, but he does try to honor Andy's wishes to raise his son as he sees fit.

I often wonder if Mr. Dave's experience with Opie caused him to rethink his lifestyle. Did he worry about the example that he was setting, or did he continue to be concerned only with his own happiness? Did it cause him to stop and think about all the things he could accomplish if he would just incorporate responsibility into his life, or did he go along his merry way drifting from one day to the next? Yes, this episode makes me think about my example to those who look up to me, but it also makes me think about my personal attitude toward my own life. Like Mr. Dave, am I content to drift from one situation to another, to just live off my wits? Or, am I prepared to make my life count, to define my goals, and to work hard to realize those goals? It's a tough choice to make because it's tempting to take the easy road. When you consider the stakes involved, however, the right choice is obvious.

CHAPTER 10

HOW DO I LOVE THEE?

"Barney and Thelma Lou, Phfft!"

Do nothing out of selfish ambition or vain conceit, but in humility consider others better than yourselves.

Philippians 2:3

Barney Fife was a character of many talents. One talent he was particularly proud of was his ability to get along with the ladies! The series is full of episodes where Barney shows us his wisdom and ways in dealing with members of the opposite sex. Barney may not have always been successful at the dating game, but he sure provided us with a lot of lasting memories! Most fans will remember Barney's most steady girlfriend, Thelma Lou. I think we can actually learn something with respect to our romantic relationships from one episode.

As the title suggests, "Barney and Thelma Lou, Phfft!" sets us up for some relationship fireworks. It seems that Barney and Thelma Lou have been dating for quite some time. The episode opens with the couple admiring furniture while window shopping. Thelma Lou is impressed with the formal living room couch while Barney is taken with the leather chair. One thing leads to another, and they begin talking about how it would be to set up a home together. Barney begins to get cold feet and he hurriedly changes the subject, but it is obvious that the two have a loving relationship and both would like to get married . . . someday!

The events of the next day unfold rather quickly. Thelma Lou has a dentist appointment in the nearby town of Mount Pilot but has no way to get there. Barney can't take her in the squad car because Andy needs it for official business. By a stroke of luck, Gomer comes into the courthouse and offers to take Thelma Lou. The plans are made, and Andy pokes a little fun at Barney by asking him if he should get a chaperone for Gomer and Thelma Lou. Barney laughs sarcastically and makes a bold statement about Thelma Lou, that he has that little girl in his hip pocket.

Well, you can probably see where this is going. Gomer hears what Barney says and innocently spills the quote to Thelma Lou while on the way to Mount Pilot. Thelma Lou, obviously disturbed at this revelation, plots her next move. She decides to focus her attention on Gomer in the hope that it will make Barney jealous. This performance turns into a huge turmoil between Barney, Gomer, and Thelma Lou. Barney is mad at Gomer because he thinks Gomer stole his girl. Thelma Lou thinks she is getting back at Barney, and poor Gomer doesn't know what to do because he hasn't a clue as to what is going on. To make matters even worse, Gomer, coming from a really conservative family, feels a commitment to marry Thelma Lou because she kissed him on the cheek. As Andy says, some couples don't even hold hands in public until their seventh or eighth young 'un comes along.

The whole scandal is a result of a lack of appreciation, maybe even a lack of respect. Barney's attitude toward Thelma Lou was not reflective of someone who really cared about her. He just assumed that, no matter what, she would always be there. And from Thelma Lou's reaction, Barney got a little taste of what life would be like without her. In the end, Thelma Lou apologizes to Gomer and to Barney for her little scheme. Her only request is that Barney never say that he has her in his hip pocket again. No matter how much we might deny it, feeling appreciated is important to us. Whether it be as a parent, a coworker, or a spouse, we all want to feel appreciated. From the other side of the equation, this episode reminds me how important it is to show my loved ones how much I appreciate them.

Since I became an engineer in 1988, my job has required me to travel. Sometimes the destinations are exciting, such as Orlando, Florida; Monterey, California; and Munich, Germany. More often than not, the destinations aren't quite so flashy. I've never heard anyone brag about going to Killeen, Texas; Leavenworth, Kansas; or Anniston, Alabama. Traveling offers several new experiences, and it can be a lot of fun. Apart from the business, there is usually a local culture to experience. I do have to admit that when I'm traveling for work, I don't always think about home that much. I am usually caught up with so many meetings and distractions, it's easy to forget about what is going on back home.

That all changes when my wife, Nicole, travels. It makes a huge difference when she is away and I'm the one left at home. The ego that goes with upgrading to first class on the plane and requesting the room with the king bed is gone. The preoccupation with a hard day's work on site then a social time after work is replaced with going home to an empty house. When you're on the road, you don't always realize how lonely it can be back at home. When you're concerned with the status of the new contract or how well the first day of software integration went, you don't remember how little fun it is to wash the clothes and keep the house straight by yourself. When you receive the praises and accolades from the customer for a job well done, it's easy to forget how hard it is to get to sleep when you're at home in your bed, alone.

When Nicole travels, it makes me appreciate her that much more. I realize how much she puts up with when I'm gone. She is in charge of the house and makes a special effort to keep everything running smoothly. I realize very quickly while I'm out "saving the world," that she is at home doing the real work. Taking someone for granted is an easy thing to do, but something that becomes very obvious when the roles are reversed.

Barney had gotten very used to Thelma Lou being there for him—so much so that he bragged that nothing could cause him to lose her. He later found out what it was like not to have Thelma Lou around, and it made him realize just how much he needed her. In our relationships, it is very easy to let our pride get in the way. We assume that we are just about the most important person there is, and that those around us should treat us as such. But it is a humbling experience to think about how our lives would be without the ones we love, without the ones we depend on every single day—the ones we so often take for granted.

CHAPTER 11

WHAT'S YOUR HURRY?

"The Sermon for Today"

Do not be anxious about anything, but in everything, by prayer and petition, with thanksgiving, present your requests to God. And the peace of God, which transcends all understanding, will guard your hearts and your minds in Christ Jesus.

Philippians 4:6–7

If you can see only one episode of *The Andy Griffith Show*, this is the one. This is one of the few episodes that actually shows the residents of Mayberry in church. From the sign outside, we can see that it is the All Souls Church. I think that if I were passing through a small town and saw the All Souls Church, I would be very tempted to stop and see what it was all about! The episode opens with Andy, Opie, and Aunt Bee at home trying to get ready for services. I'm sure it is a familiar scene to a lot of us with Opie still in his pajamas, Aunt Bee trying to get ready, and Andy yelling, "We're going to be late." I remember similar Sunday mornings at our house with my mom and dad and four of us kids struggling to get ready on time. My dad was not one to yell about the time, but he did have a particular habit. As the time to leave approached, we would be running around the house trying to find socks, shoes, and whatever else we needed. My dad was nowhere to be found. Instead of waiting inside and watching all the confusion, he would just get in the car and wait. No yelling or horn blowing, he would just wait in the car. After a while, we didn't have to look at the clock to see if we were running late. If Dad wasn't in the house, we knew it was time to go.

I've got to believe that the episode, "The Sermon for Today," was a lot of fun to make, especially the scene in the church building. On this particular Sunday morning, the All Souls Church has a guest speaker, Dr. Harrison Everett Breen from New York City. Dr. Breen, a friend of the regular pastor, Reverend Tucker, has graciously offered to deliver the morning's lesson. We get to experience several aspects of a traditional service in this episode along with some comical events we can all relate to, like Barney singing then forgetting the words and having to look on Andy's hymnal. Then Opie catches a fly in his hand. Finally, who can forget Gomer falling asleep during the sermon, and to everyone's horror, he actually starts snoring.

What I want to highlight is Dr. Breen's sermon itself, because Dr. Breen preaches about the advantages of a simpler lifestyle. A curious sermon for the people of Mayberry.

Dr. Breen's Sermon:

As I stood there during the singing of the hymn, I asked myself, "What message have I to bring these good people

of Mayberry?" And I was reminded of an instance. A
young man came to me recently and said he: "Dr. Breen,
what is the meaning of it all?" And I said to him, "Young
man, I'm glad you asked." My friends, I wish more of us
found the time to ask that question. Whither . . . whither
are we headed and why? Why this senseless rush, this
mad pursuit, this frantic competition, this pace that kills?
Why do we drive ourselves as we do? In our furious race
these days to conquer outer space, are we not perhaps
forgetting inner space? Shall we find the true meaning of
life by fleeing from it?

Consider . . . consider how we live our lives today.
Everything is run, run, run. We bolt our breakfast, we
scan the headlines, we race to the office. The full schedule
and the split second: these are our gauges of success. We
drive ourselves from morn to night. We have forgotten the
meaning of the word relaxation. What has become of the
old-fashioned ways, the simple pleasures of the past?

Who can forget, for example, the old-fashioned band concert at twilight on the village green. The joy, the serenity
of just sitting and listening. This is lost to us, and this we
should strive to recapture, a simple innocent pleasure.

And so I say to you, dear friends, relax . . . slow down . . .
take it easy . . .

What's your hurry!?

What indeed, friends, is your hurry?

Let me just stop here and say that I can't give you a fitting description of what happens with Dr. Breen's last words, but I'll try. As Dr. Breen is winding down, he speaks in a very soft and comforting voice; "Slow down . . . take it easy . . ." At this point the camera is on Andy and Barney, and they are very comfortable in the pew. They appear to be relaxed and even a little sleepy. Just when they are totally at ease, Dr.

Breen continues by bellowing, "What's your hurry!!!" The startled expressions of Andy and Barney are priceless!

"Why on earth would the citizens of Mayberry need to hear a sermon like that?" you might ask. After all, Mayberry is the epitome of the simpler lifestyle. Just the mention of Mayberry conjures up images of sitting on the front porch while Andy plays the guitar or stopping by the courthouse to have a cup of coffee with Barney. This particular sermon had a strange effect on the townspeople of Mayberry. In their attempt to follow Dr. Breen's advice, they almost ended up doing themselves in.

After Sunday dinner, Aunt Bee, Andy, and Barney begin to reflect on Dr. Breen's sermon. They discuss how nice it would be to revive the old band concerts. Before you know it, Andy has the band together practicing, Aunt Bee and Clara are working on the uniforms, and Barney has sought the assistance of Gomer to fix up the old bandstand. However, what seemed like a simple idea after lunch turns into a major ordeal. The band members are woefully out of practice, the uniforms are torn and covered with mildew, and the bandstand is accidentally destroyed when Gomer uses a hammer to take a whack at a spider. In their efforts to revive a tradition of yesterday, the members of the gang have completely worn themselves out, and they don't even have a band concert to show for their effort.

This episode vividly illustrates the trouble we go to just to slow down our lives. We find it hard to relax, so we must have a plan or a project or somewhere to go. We can't just enjoy the peace and quiet. Using the guise of taking it easy, we end up busier than ever before. To complicate matters, we can even feel guilty about taking it easy. I know that if I find myself with some spare time, I feel like I need to be doing something. I need to be getting something accomplished. If we always have this attitude, when will we ever take the time to slow down?

I believe that finding the time to relax is something we have lost in our current society, and I can think of at least a couple of reasons why we tend to have that attitude. First, we are told from an early age that our professional success is everything and that we should put all our time and effort into being successful in the business world. As Dr. Breen said, the full schedule and the split second are the measures of our success. But do these things really measure the success in a person's life? I know many people who are very successful in the business world, but some of these same people have very little happiness or success in any other aspect of their lives. Another myth we believe is that we must be involved in an activity in order to relax. The few precious moments we allow in our schedules for personal time are cluttered with events. For some reason, just the thought of not doing anything at all can make us feel uncomfortable.

How often do we take the time just to stop and really appreciate the simple things of life? I would suggest that for our own spiritual, mental, and physical health, we should make a conscious effort to plan specific times to relax. By relaxing I do not mean participating in a sporting event or even a band concert, but a time when we take a break from all the world's activities and meditate on what is really important in our lives. That is, a time to spend with ourselves, our families, and our God. If it is important enough to us, we will make the time. So, as Dr. Breen said, don't be afraid to relax and slow down. It may be just what you need.

CHAPTER 12
GOOD LUCK

"The Jinx"

Some trust in chariots and some in horses, but we trust in the name of the LORD our God.

Psalm 20:7

I think we've all known a Henry Bennett at one time or another. In fact, sometimes I think I am Henry Bennett. Henry is a nice enough gentleman in Mayberry, but it seems that wherever Henry goes, bad luck follows. The jinx discussion starts in Floyd's barbershop when Barney blames his loss at checkers on the fact that Henry is standing over his shoulder. Floyd also chimes in saying that his son missed a fly ball at a recent baseball game right after Henry returned a foul ball. Andy reminds Floyd that his son missed the only ball hit to him during the entire game. At this point, Andy decides to put an end to the jinx talk by inviting Henry to join him and Barney in the opening day fishing sweepstakes. Barney and Andy have won the sweepstakes for the past few years, so this is a perfect opportunity to dispel any rumors that Henry is a jinx.

Barney is horrified that Henry will be in their boat. To ward off any bad luck, Barney consults his book of lucky charms and chants. Barney even rubs Opie's head because he reads that rubbing the head of a red-haired boy is lucky. The day of the fishing sweepstakes arrives and Andy, Barney, and Henry set out in the boat together. Barney still insists that they are doomed, and he continues his attempts to combat Henry's bad luck by saying more chants and rubbing a rabbit's foot. Finally, Andy hooks a big one. Henry is ecstatic that his string of bad luck is over, but suddenly the boat springs a leak. The boat sinks and so does Henry's hope that his bad luck is gone.

After the disaster at the fishing hole, Henry actually believes that he is a jinx. Furthermore, Henry believes that the

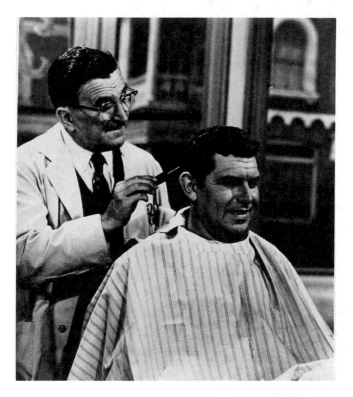

best thing he can do is leave town. Almost in tears, he arrives at the barbershop to tell the boys that he doesn't want to be held responsible for all the bad things that happen in Mayberry. After Henry leaves, the shop is silent. Floyd, Barney, and the rest of the boys realize what they have done with all the talk about bad luck and jinxes. Andy is ashamed of their behavior and asks if they really believe Henry is a jinx—enough so that they actually want him to leave town.

Barney and Floyd come to their senses and admit that they don't really believe Henry is a jinx. They know that the bad things that happened were just coincidental, but the fact remains that they still said some very hurtful things to Henry. Only Henry's sudden announcement makes them stop long enough to realize what they were doing. Fortunately, it's not too late. The citizens of Mayberry want Henry to stay so badly that they rig a door prize at the Saturday night dance just so Henry will win and realize that his luck has changed. Henry almost botches the drawing by selecting the hat size instead of the winning number (they were all winning numbers), but the townspeople give the prize to Henry anyway. Henry, reminded that he is indeed a fortunate man to have so many friends who care about him, decides to stay put in Mayberry.

Barney is in rare form in this episode. A memorable scene takes place in the boat when he comes up with some hilarious chants to ward off bad luck. It makes me consider all the things in our lives that we attribute to luck. I wonder, are we really that superstitious? I don't think there is anything wrong with wishing someone good luck, but do we really attribute our success to luck, or is our faith seated in something deeper?

I will always be indebted to my cousin, Mark Harless, who reintroduced me to *The Andy Griffith Show* while I was attending college. Mark has a very outgoing personality and a vivid imagination. One might even say he is a little superstitious. As we both became young professionals, we began to travel with our respective companies. One day we were talking about the adventures and perils of air travel, and Mark shared with me a "tradition" he always performed when entering an aircraft. He said he would always touch the exterior of the plane as he entered the door for good luck. Well, that sounded good to me. After all, Mark had never been in a serious aircraft incident, so it couldn't hurt.

As my travel schedule increased, I began to find myself touching the exterior of the plane every time I went onboard. I must have made a little more ceremony of it than just a casual touch because on one occasion I had a fellow passenger ask me why I touched the plane like that. Feeling a little embarrassed, I explained that it was good luck. He looked at me, thought for a minute, then went back and touched the plane himself. I continued this practice for quite awhile and didn't think much about it. My rule was: if I was going to get on a plane, I was going to touch the outside before I got on. My good luck insurance seemed to work pretty well until I made a trip to Washington, D.C. on May 8, 1995.

The flight from Atlanta to D.C. began just fine. I was in a great mood because I was able to upgrade to first class with a frequent flyer coupon. I was seated comfortably with my real (not Styrofoam) coffee cup and was going over my notes for a briefing that I had later in the day. Everything was quiet and smooth until "BOOM." After the boom the whole plane shuddered violently and immediately began to lose altitude. The "fasten seatbelt" sign came on, and the flight attendants turned very serious and began securing the cabin. At that point my briefing and nice cup of coffee seemed very unimportant. After a few minutes the captain came on the radio. Let me mention that when the captain begins with "Ladies and Gentlemen, we have an update on the situation . . . " it doesn't instill a lot of confidence. Apparently the right engine had literally exploded. The good news (if there is such a thing with an engine explosion) was that the engine was still intact and had been shut down safely, and there was no fire. I'm a bit of an aviation buff so I knew that the aircraft we were on was a Boeing 757. I also knew that the Boeing 757 had two engines. One of our engines was now dead. We all hoped that the engine problem was not contagious. The captain told us that we were making a rapid descent to make an emergency landing somewhere in North Carolina. That was the last we heard from him during the flight.

The time it took the plane to go from 33,000 feet to the airport was about twenty minutes, the longest twenty minutes of my life. During that time my priorities changed drastically. I was no longer worried about work or sitting in first class. I wasn't concerned if my luggage would make it or if the hotel was going to be nice. I also wasn't trying to think of good luck charms or chants that I could say to get us out of this mess. The fact that I had touched this plane for good luck before boarding was a distant memory. I was painfully aware that I had no control of the situation at all.

It probably comes as no surprise that I used my twenty minutes to pray, and I'm sure that most of the other passengers and flight crew did so as well. The entire cabin was completely quiet. The conversation and laughter of just a few minutes ago had been replaced with blank stares out the window or heads slightly bowed.

I prayed for the pilot, I prayed for the aircraft, and I prayed that God would see all of us through this crisis. At that moment I realized just how much I relied on God for everything. Nothing else was important. All the trivial things that make up our lives meant nothing. I knew that God, and God alone, had the power to protect us.

As we approached the runway, I began to have a little more hope. The left engine showed no signs of letting up, and the captain seemed to have good control of the plane. We hit the ground pretty hard, but we made it in one piece. Without the right engine's thrust reversal, the captain did have a little trouble stopping the plane, but we did come to a stop before the end of the runway. It was an eerie sight to see all the fire engines and rescue vehicles lined up on the runway, just in case the landing hadn't turned out so well. Once we were on the ground, all the passengers let out a cheer and applauded. The crisis was over, and we were all safe. I found it ironic that soon these same thankful people would be in line at the ticket counter griping to the agents to get them to D.C., and to get them there now.

As I was walking through the airport food court, I noticed the captain of our flight sitting alone at a table with a cup of coffee. I walked up and could tell he was still a little shaken. I thanked him again for getting us down safely, and he simply replied, "Yeah, we were lucky out there today."

Funny, at that point "luck" was the farthest thing from my mind as to why we made it safely to the airport that day.

CHAPTER 13

MIRROR, MIRROR

"Deputy Otis"

You were taught, with regard to your former way of life,
to put off your old self, which is being corrupted by its
deceitful desires; to be made new in the attitude of your
minds; and to put on the new self, created to be like God
in true righteousness and holiness.

Ephesians 4:22–24

"I wonder if he's going to talk about the town drunk, Otis?"
I know some of you are asking that question, so the answer
is yes! But I'm not going to talk about the evils of drinking.
I believe the issue is a bit larger than that. Otis Campbell is
a very lovable character in Mayberry. We understand that he
has a problem but we love him anyway. We don't feel sorry
for Otis, but we see him for what he is: someone who has a
hard time resisting the temptation to drink too much.
However, I do think we need to be careful when considering
Otis because we never see the downside to his lifestyle. In
the show Otis is extremely funny when he is drunk, but we
never see the seriousness of his problem, or do we?

"Deputy Otis" gives us a little insight into how Otis really
feels about his life. Unbeknownst to Andy and Barney, Otis

has been writing to his brother, Ralph, telling him that he is a sheriff's deputy. Otis wants to make an impression that he has done something with his life, that he is respectable. This charade goes on until Ralph and his wife, Verlaine (I don't make these names up), decide to come to Mayberry for a visit. Otis is very honest with Andy and tells him about the deception. However, upon hearing Otis's story Andy offers to swear Otis in as a temporary deputy. Barney opposes the idea and even accuses Andy of "falsifying," but Andy defends his action by saying that Otis will be a deputy for only as long as his brother and sister-in-law are visiting. Back at Otis's house, Andy reminds the new deputy that it is his duty to confiscate and destroy any illegal liquor on the premises. As much as he hates it, Otis must oblige and he pours a bottle of previously hidden moonshine down the drain.

Ralph and Verlaine make it to town, and for a while Otis thinks that his plan is working. Even though Ralph suggests that the two "have a snort," Otis doesn't relent. However, later on when Otis can't find Ralph, he assumes that he has slipped off to town to find out about the real Otis. Otis goes down to the courthouse to tell Andy and Barney that the plan just didn't work.

A funny thing happens while the three are at the courthouse. Ralph, looking more like the old Otis, comes staggering in and locks himself up in a cell. You see, Otis is not the only town drunk in the family. Andy is amazed that this is the brother Otis is so worried about impressing. However, Otis's reaction is not relief; it is disgust. He can't believe that his brother would have such a flagrant disregard for the law and would act in such a manner in front of his friends. In

effect, Otis is looking at a mirror and doesn't like what he sees at all.

No matter how hard we try, we are going to struggle in certain areas of our lives. It may not be with alcohol, as in the case of Otis, but we will be tempted, and we will fail. I think the question becomes, *How do we deal with those temptations and failures?* Otis didn't want to admit he had a problem. He was content, with Andy's help, to cover his problem and act like all was well. However, Otis eventually realized that it was a futile effort. No matter how well he covered himself, the truth would eventually come out. He wasn't perfect, and he found out that his brother wasn't perfect either. I wonder how their relationship might have been different if they had just been honest with each other in the first place.

In the episode, Otis said that no one in his family ever thought that he would amount to any good. I don't know what would be worse, being told I would never amount to anything or being held to such a standard that no matter what I did it wouldn't be good enough. When I was growing up my family always encouraged me; they were never overbearing to the point that I feared going home when I messed up. They gave me the love and the freedom to make my own decisions and to learn from my failures. No matter how many times I failed, I never doubted the love and acceptance my family showed me.

Even with the environment I had growing up, it is still hard to admit that my life is not perfect. Further complicating my situation is the fact that I am somewhat of a perfectionist. I'm one of those people whose desk at work is always straight and uncluttered, and whose car is always washed and vacuumed. If you want to see me sweat, let a five-year-old with an ice cream cone ride in the backseat of my car for a while. However, life is rarely as uncluttered as I like my surroundings to be. No matter how much it bothers me, there is no area in my life that is perfect.

When you consider how we tend to act around each other, you would think that we all have perfect lives. When we see each other, we talk about how great our jobs are going and how successful we have been. We tell each other that everything is fine and the family is doing great. We seem to be afraid to tell the truth because we will be perceived as having problems or not living up to expectations. If we were willing to share more, we would realize that our problems are not unique and, in fact, are very similar to the problems experienced by those around us. But this pressure to be perfect keeps our walls up, and we continue the façade.

Last year Nicole and I took a class aimed at improving marriages. The course was based on meeting each other's needs and offered some very practical suggestions on how to take the focus off yourself and direct that energy toward your spouse. We attended the class with several couples we knew, some we had known for a long time. Probably one of the biggest impressions I gained from that class was that everyone had problems. I think we lose sight of this fact when we give the appearance that everything is fine. This class forced all of us to drop the act and really discuss some of the serious issues in our lives. As we went through the class, we started forming bonds with each other because we realized that we were more alike than we thought. Instead of thinking that we really must be in trouble because nobody else could possibly be struggling with the same issues, we realized we were not alone.

Admitting that you are not perfect is not easy. It takes courage and faith, especially if you've been burned by people who have used your weaknesses against you. But the strength and encouragement we receive by sharing and by opening our hearts to others far outweighs the risk and apprehension involved. We need to be people who are not afraid to admit our weaknesses, but we also need to be willing to accept others for who they are. When we have that attitude of acceptance, I believe that we will be able to see others as Christ sees us—with love, patience, and understanding.

CHAPTER 14

YOU CAN'T STAY HERE

"Mayberry Goes Bankrupt"

In everything I did, I showed you that by this kind of hard work we must help the weak, remembering the words the Lord Jesus himself said: "It is more blessed to give than to receive."

Acts 20:35

We've all seen it. You know where it is—especially if you live in a small town. It's the one house everyone sees as the town's disgrace. The one lot with cars in the front yard that haven't moved in years, grass that rarely gets mowed, and shrubs that are never trimmed. It's the house we look at and wonder why the owners don't do something with the place. The eyesore of the neighborhood. The one we pass by and just shake our heads.

Mayberry has a house like that too. The yard is a mess. The fence is dilapidated. The house needs painting and the roof needs fixing. It's owned by a nice old man named Frank Myers. It seems that Frank is in the berry business. That is, he has a huge collection of fake berries that he uses to create women's hats. Unfortunately, berries aren't in style right now. If they ever do come back in style, Frank will be sitting on a gold mine. In the meantime, Frank is having problems making ends meet. He wasn't able to pay his taxes, so the town council decided to foreclose on his house. After all, it is a dump. It's the scourge of Mayberry. The faster they get Frank out, the council members reason, the quicker they can do something with the property to make it more presentable.

At the town council meeting, the mayor and the rest of the council members elect Andy to serve the eviction notice to Frank. Andy is against the idea, but he knows that he is outnumbered. Andy states that this is one part of sheriffing he can do without. Andy complies, however, and takes the news to Frank who isn't really surprised. He knew that he was behind on his taxes, but he just kept hoping to catch a break. It seems that his break is never going to come. Andy says something about trying to delay the council's actions, but his statement sounds kind of weak even to Andy. Andy has no solution to the problem, so he does his duty. He serves the eviction notice. Frank accepts it, and he tells the sheriff he is glad that Andy is the one who delivered the notice. In an uncomfortable moment, it's good to have a friend close by.

Later, back on the Taylor's front porch, Andy is feeling really bad about what he has been called to do. He complains about the mayor and the town council and how stubborn they are. Andy and Aunt Bee recall their friendship with Frank and how it is a shame that this has happened to such a nice person. Such a shame indeed. The conversation would have probably ended there if it weren't for Opie.

Opie asks Andy what *evicted* means. Andy explains the term, and then Opie asks where Frank will go since he doesn't have a house anymore. Andy further explains that Frank will probably go to stay with friends or family or something like that. Opie then asks Andy if he means friends like themselves. Andy and Aunt Bee slowly begin to realize that Opie is suggesting that Frank come and stay with the Taylors for a while. At first Andy and Aunt Bee are hesitant. Why, you can't just ask somebody to come stay with you, or can you? Then it all makes sense. It is so simple. Identifying a need and meeting it right there on the spot.

I often wonder why it took Opie to make the suggestion. It would seem that Andy and Aunt Bee would be more aware of Frank's immediate needs than Opie. However, Opie knew enough to know that Frank needed a place to stay. He also knew that they had an extra bedroom, and he felt at least partly responsible for Frank's predicament because his pa served him the eviction notice. Even though Andy and Aunt Bee both cared for Frank and were distraught about the situation, it never dawned on either of them to invite Frank into their home. As I watch this scene, I wonder if my reaction would be like Opie's or like Andy's. Would I immediately see the opportunity, or would I just sigh and think to myself how life sure is unfair.

Sometimes I think we have programmed ourselves right out of our responsibility to each other. We are fortunate enough to live in a country where the needs of the less fortunate are very much a priority. The government has implemented welfare programs for years. I also believe our churches do a very good job at tending to the needs of the community. But how willing are we as individuals to make the personal sacrifice to help someone in need? Do we just assume that someone else will step in and assist the person, or do we, like Opie, take an active role in helping the person ourselves?

When you think about it, it is much easier to give money to a worthy program than it is to really get involved. But is that really what Jesus is talking about in Matthew when he states that the ones who will inherit eternal life are the same ones who tend to "the least of these" while here on this earth? Usually it does take some sacrifice for us to help someone in need. It might take of our time and energy, and chances are we will be inconvenienced in some way. But will we even see the opportunity to help unless we are specifically looking for it? We can be so involved with our own lives and schedules that we may never see the Frank Myers of our society.

After Frank arrived at Andy's house, they were going through some of Frank's valuables when they found a hundred-year-old bond that was purchased by his grandfather from the town of Mayberry. With compounding interest, the value of the bond was calculated to be worth over a quarter of a million dollars. Since the town obviously couldn't pay the bond, the now compassionate town council decided it would be appropriate to fix up Frank's house, that is, until they realized that the bond was purchased when Mayberry was part of the Confederacy. Since the bond was bought with Confederate money, it was worthless. As you can imagine, the council members immediately lost their newfound compassion and once again demanded that Frank be evicted. Fortunately, Andy was able to convince the council members that they had just done something nice for a neighbor and should leave it at that.

That short scene on the front porch with Opie, Andy, and Aunt Bee was fairly insignificant with respect to the rest of the episode, but I think it speaks volumes to our general attitude toward those in need. It is easy to assume that somebody else will take care of the situation or that the person in need will make it somehow. It's much harder to really notice the opportunity to serve and to take a genuine interest. Is it really that hard? Maybe it just requires the ability to see those situations through the eyes of a child, just like Opie saw Frank.

CHAPTER 15

THE EMPTY CAGE

"Opie the Birdman"

But those who hope in the LORD will renew their strength.
They will soar on wings like eagles;
they will run and not grow weary,
they will walk and not be faint.

Isaiah 40:31

"Opie the Birdman" is my favorite episode of the entire *Andy Griffith Show* series. If you were to ask me why it is my favorite, I don't know that I could tell you. There are funnier episodes, more touching episodes, and maybe even episodes that have a more powerful message. But this one is special. If you've seen it, you will probably agree.

The episode begins with Opie putting together a slingshot. Andy, Barney, and Opie are in the courthouse, and Barney is attempting to show Opie how to use the ancient weapon. Barney explains that such devices were used way back in biblical times, referring to David and Goliath, but Barney becomes confused when Opie asks where David got the rubber for the sling. Barney begins to say that David just cut up an old tire, but he stops himself in time. Andy, on the other hand, tells Opie to have fun with the slingshot but to be careful with it.

Opie promises his pa that he will be careful and goes on his way shooting at tin cans and other stuff. When he gets to his house, Opie hears a noise in one of the trees in the front yard. Without hesitation, he shoots toward the noise. Opie watches in amazement as a little bird plunges to the ground. At first, he doesn't want to believe what has happened. He begs for the bird to fly, pleads for it to fly, but all to no avail. Finally, he runs into the house sobbing. Later that evening, Andy confronts Opie about the bird. Opie admits that he killed the bird but he didn't mean to. He tells Andy that he is sorry. Andy responds by saying that being sorry isn't the magic word that makes everything right again. Actions bring consequences, and the bird Opie killed was a mother. Three baby birds are now crying for their mother who is not coming back.

At this point Opie has a decision to make. He can wallow in his guilt, or he can do something to make the situation better. Although he can't bring the mother bird back, he can do something for her babies. Opie takes it upon himself to care for the little birds and puts much effort into raising them the best way he can. At the end of the show, Opie has to make the hard decision to let the birds go. He knows he has done everything he can to ensure that the birds will be all right, but he is still not sure he has done all the right things until the moment he releases each bird. When the three birds are gone, Opie looks at the cage and comments how empty it now looks. Andy agrees that the cage does seem empty, but he points out how full the trees now seem with their new singing residents. Because of Opie, a tragic story had a wonderful ending.

One reason this episode is special to me is because it reminds me that life doesn't always happen as I expect it to.

Opie didn't mean for the mother bird to die, but she did. Even though he was sincerely sorry, it didn't change the fact that the mother was gone and that he now had a responsibility to the little ones left behind. At the time, Opie was crushed. All he could do was run to his room in tears. He didn't know what to do or how to handle the situation. Even when he decided to care for the birds, he didn't know what to do next. He just took it a day at a time and did the best he could. Slowly, it became apparent that he was doing some things right because the birds were getting stronger. However, it wasn't until he actually released the birds that he knew he had succeeded. Up until that point, he just relied on faith that everything would work out.

On a grander scale, I see our lives in a similar way. We are handed situations, and it is up to us to deal with them. Most of the time we don't have any idea of the first step to take, much less what the outcome will be. Our only choice is to take it one day at a time and do the very best we can. Sometimes all we have to rely on is the promise that all things work together for good.

****

She was thirty-three years old. A mother of two beautiful boys and a faithful Christian woman. However, her husband, Mike, would have told you that she was the mother of three boys. She probably would have agreed. Bonnie and Mike loved working with kids. They both were very active in the youth program at their church long before their own kids came along. They even spent part of their honeymoon chaperoning a youth retreat. Now that is dedication and love. Bonnie and Mike were truly partners. They relied on each other to get the job done. They each pulled their own weight and didn't complain. They loved the Lord, loved their kids, and loved each other.

On August 22, 1999, Bonnie was taken from us. She had injured her ankle a few weeks earlier, and during the recovery process a blood clot had formed. On that Sunday morning she woke up with shortness of breath. After the paramedics came she was feeling better, but the situation changed drastically once she got in the ambulance. The blood clot had moved into her lung, and she died.

This isn't supposed to happen. Healthy thirty-three-year-old mothers are not supposed to die. We can only ask why. Why did this happen? Why did God take the mother of those two young boys? Why would God want the father to raise his sons alone? It doesn't make sense. It doesn't make any sense at all.

Our lives are filled with trouble, and when we look at the Scriptures, we find that this reality has been present in the human condition for a long time. The story of Job gives us a stark picture of how a good life on this earth can go bad very quickly. Sometimes I think we have the idea that if we are Christians nothing bad will ever happen to us. But upon closer examination, we are never given that promise. However, we are given the assurance that we will not have to face the struggles and trials of our lives alone.

As I grow older, I begin to realize how we as humans have the ability to cope. Sometimes terrible things happen, and if we had the foreknowledge of these events, we would say that we could never handle them. However, they do happen, and we do handle them. We handle them by relying on God, on our friends and families, and on the fact that we are not permanent residents of this world. Sometimes tragic events remind us that this life is very short and that each day we are given should be treated as a great blessing.

What good can you see from such a tragic event? We can see life for what it really is—a temporary journey on a planet whose days are numbered. An opportunity for us to serve one another. The realization that we are called to a higher standard and will answer for our lives one day. An opportunity to tell our loved ones how we feel about them. An adjustment of priorities. A realization of our destiny.

It shouldn't have happened. Thirty-three-year-olds are not supposed to die. However, there was another thirty-three-year-old who died so innocently. He was in the prime of His life, and He did nothing to deserve the fate He had to endure. But He wasn't concerned for Himself. It wasn't His life that He was concerned about saving.

It shouldn't have happened, but it did. And because He died, all of humanity has hope.

CHAPTER 16

TRUTH IN ADVERTISING

"Barney Fife, Realtor"

For God, who said, "Let light shine out of darkness,"
made his light shine in our hearts to give us the light of
the knowledge of the glory of God in the face of Christ.
But we have this treasure in jars of clay to show that this
all-surpassing power is from God and not from us.

2 Corinthians 4:6–7

By the title, you might wonder what lesson can be taken from the episode "Barney Fife, Realtor." In this episode, Barney has obviously taken up the real estate game and is already seeing dollar signs. He tries to talk Andy into looking at a larger house, but at first Andy is not interested. However, after more prompting Andy reconsiders and tells Barney he would like to look at the new house. This action throws Barney into a frenzy, and he immediately finds a prospective buyer for Andy's house. Barney figures that the more people he can move, the more money he will make.

An important scene in this episode is when Andy finds Opie attempting to sell his bike to his friend, Howie. Andy asks Opie if he has come clean with all the problems with the bike. Opie had not originally planned to tell Howie that the innertubes were full of patches and the chain had been fixed with wire. Opie questions whether he should have to disclose all the problems with the bike or just assume a "buyer beware" attitude. Andy tells Opie that he should always be honest when dealing with others.

Fast-forward to Barney the realtor. He has the prospective buyers, the Simses, ready to see the Taylors' house. To Barney's dismay, Opie points out several problems with the house in front of the Simses. The evening turns out to be a disaster, and the Simses end up leaving quickly. Andy is convinced that the reason Opie pointed out the flaws is to get back at him for ruining the bike deal. However, upon further examination Andy realizes that Opie has a legitimate question: Are there different rules for kids and grownups as far as honesty is concerned? At first Andy has trouble answering this question. In the meantime, Barney convinces the Simses to take another look at the house, explaining that Opie has a rather active imagination. Barney states that the problems with the house aren't that serious.

Andy now has a choice to make. He can either agree with Barney and dismiss the problems Opie pointed out, or he can be a powerful example to his son by admitting that Opie was pretty much on the mark. Of course, Andy does the right thing and tells the Simses that the house is not perfect; that problems do exist. The telling scene here is Opie's reaction. You can see the relief on Opie's face as he realizes that his father does indeed practice what he preaches.

This episode is a pointed lesson on honesty. The scene in which Andy is trying to explain to Opie the difference between houses and bikes is classic. The conversation is obviously uncomfortable for Andy because he begins to realize he can't explain why Opie should come clean with the problems with his bike when he isn't going to be forthcoming with the house's imperfections. In the end, it was just a matter of being honest. But there is another lesson, perhaps not quite as obvious, but important just the same. When the Simses first came to see the Taylors' house, Andy and Aunt Bee were careful to try to cover up all the flaws. They didn't want to admit that the house had problems. Sometimes I think we can have that attitude in our lives as well. It can involve anything in our lives that we don't want to admit is not perfect. Our marriages, our relationships, they all have cracks. But to what extent do we go to hide those cracks so they won't be seen by others?

Shortly after we bought our current home, the house next door went up for sale. A few months passed and the house remained empty. One spring afternoon we heard a knock at the back door. A very friendly man named Bobby and his wife, Diane, had been looking at the house and wanted to meet a few of the neighbors. Bobby, Diane, Nicole, and I immediately hit it off and spent quite a bit of time talking about the neighborhood, the house, etc. After they left, we definitely knew we would love to have these people as our neighbors.

A couple of weeks went by and our hope that Bobby and Diane were still interested in the house began to fade. However, one Sunday afternoon as I was leaving to go to town, Bobby and Diane returned with a realtor to take another look at the house. I stopped to say hello, and that's when the yapping started. Nicole and I are the owners of

two very large Dalmatians, and no matter how they are por-
trayed in the movies, Dalmatians aren't nearly as smart or
well-behaved as you might think. Anyway, I had started my
truck, and both dogs began to whine to go for a ride. The
longer I talked, the more those two sounded like a couple of
hyenas. The male dog, Dylan, wasn't barking; he was emit-
ting this high-pitched whine that sounded more like the
mating call of a tropical bird. The female, Samantha, was
trying to whine, but she sounded more like a sick cow.

Not wanting the new couple to get the wrong idea about
our perfectly behaved mutts, I quickly let them out of the
backyard and put them on our elevated deck to keep them
quiet. It was a nice day so I told Nicole to keep an eye on them
for as long as the couple was looking at the house, and then
she could put them back in the yard. Again, my intent was to
remove any idea that our dogs would ever be a nuisance.

When I returned home a few hours later, I casually asked
how long Bobby and Diane had stayed at the house next
door. Nicole just looked at me. After asking her what was
wrong, she related a story so ridiculous it had to be true.
Apparently Bobby and Diane really gave the house a once
over, and they ended up staying well over an hour. During
this time, the dogs began to get restless. Nicole decided
enough was enough so she let the dogs go down the deck
stairs to put them up in the backyard. Once the dogs
reached the bottom of the stairs, they immediately noticed
the new people at the other house. They also noticed the
open garage door at the other house. Before Nicole got to
the bottom step, Samantha and Dylan were in hot pursuit
of the new people. However, they didn't stop at the new
people. They ran past the new people and into the open

garage. Interestingly enough, the door from the garage to the interior of the house happened to be open as well. So, Samantha and Dylan continued their race into the house. All this time, Nicole was giving chase and screaming at the top of her lungs for the dogs to come back. By the time Nicole got to the house, the dogs were running amuck through every room downstairs. Dylan was on his way up the stairs to the second floor when she arrived. At this point, even an animal as dense as a Dalmatian knows he is in trouble. However, instead of heeding Nicole's commands to return to the yard, they just sat down, right where they were, on the spot.

Nicole was now faced with the task of dragging two seventy-five-pound dogs by the collar out of a house she does not own, in front of a very surprised realtor she does not know and two very nice people who wouldn't buy this house if their lives depended on it. As I sat there with my mouth open, I could not believe what I had just heard. My whole point in moving the dogs to the deck was to ensure that our prospective neighbors wouldn't get the wrong impression of our silly dogs. But now they surely thought the two canines were wild bohemians.

We all want to make good impressions; but sometimes we can try too hard to create those impressions, and sometimes the impressions we try to create aren't really all that accurate if we're honest with ourselves. In this episode, Andy was also trying to create an impression for Barney the realtor and the two prospective buyers. He wanted them to think that his house was perfect. I wanted Bobby and Diane to think that our neighborhood was perfect, including our dogs. Andy realized his mistake and was honest about the flaws in his house. This example of truthfulness and honesty was not lost by Opie. His father's actions made the real impression.

Worrying about appearances isn't limited to houses. Appearances are important to us as people. What is more important, however, is to be honest—to be able to admit that we're not perfect and that we have flaws. After all, how successful are we at covering our imperfections? We may be able to fool people for a while, but the truth will eventually come out. It would seem a lot less trouble just to admit that we aren't perfect and let people see us for who we really are. And in most cases, I believe people will like the real us better anyway.

What happened to Bobby and Diane? They bought the house anyway, and the six of us are getting along just fine!

CHAPTER 17

DIVIDED WE FALL

"A Feud is a Feud"

May the God who gives endurance and encouragement
give you a spirit of unity among yourselves as you follow
Christ Jesus, so that with one heart and mouth you may
glorify the God and Father of our Lord Jesus Christ.

Romans 15:5–6

You've heard of the Hatfields and McCoys. Well, be prepared to meet the Wakefields and the Carters. In the episode "A Feud is a Feud" the Wakefield and Carter families have been feuding for more than eighty-seven years. However, Hannah Wakefield and Josh Carter have fallen in love, and they want Andy to marry them in the middle of the night. A sleepy Andy is happy to oblige until he realizes just who they are. To make matters worse, both Hannah and Josh's fathers burst into Andy's living room donning shotguns and demanding that the marriage be stopped. Conceding to the gun-bearing papas, Andy halts the wedding.

The next morning Opie and Aunt Bee are a little perturbed at Andy. They feel that Andy let Mr. Carter and Mr. Wakefield push him around. They think that Andy should not be intimidated by the fathers and should perform the

ceremony for Josh and Hannah. Andy does support Josh and Hannah, but he wants to find out a little more about the feud that has kept the families apart for so many years. In a memorable scene, Andy tells Opie his own version of Romeo and Juliet. Andy concludes by telling Opie that he will try to get to the bottom of the feud so that Josh and Hannah won't end up like the loving couple in that classic story.

Upon further investigation, Andy realizes that neither Mr. Carter nor Mr. Wakefield have any idea why the two families are feuding. They both admit that the feud has been going on for so long that there is no one left who knows the feud's origin. Andy's plan is to end the feud once and for all by staging an old-fashioned duel between Mr. Carter and Mr. Wakefield. Andy knows that the men have no real reason to dislike each other, but to make sure everyone is safe, he secretly empties the shotguns before the men duel. As expected, Carter and Wakefield back down from the duel, but now they're concerned about being such cowards that a union of the two families could only produce a "coward's coward." Andy reminds the men of the courage it took for Josh and Hannah to stand up to their fathers, and is able to convince the men that any grandchild from the marriage would be just as courageous. Carter and Wakefield see the advantages of their families' union and both consent to the marriage.

This episode presents a clear example of how petty differences can be so divisive. The Carters and Wakefields had no idea why they were feuding; they just knew from their history that they were supposed to hate each other. I wonder if we, as believers, can be guilty of the same thing. Before I continue, I want to say that I'm not trying to trivialize the issue of doctrinal differences, but I am suggesting that we try to find common ground upon which we all can agree. Surely unity is worth something. Several years ago I attended a Promise Keepers convention in Atlanta. At one point the speaker asked all fifty thousand of us to shout the name of the church or denomination we belonged to. We all shouted our individual church names, and the sound came out as an unrecognizable blurb. The speaker then asked us to shout the name of our Lord and Savior, and at the same time every man in the assembly shouted the name "Jesus." This time the message was clear as a bell. Even though we had come from different backgrounds and beliefs, we obviously had one thing in common.

Though simple, that exercise at the convention had a powerful message. It caused me to realize that when our focus is on God, we are unified. However, when we are concerned with the matters of men, our unity begins to fail. We can get so caught up in our petty differences that we forget our purpose. If all of our time is spent arguing, how can we work together? The message also caused me to reexamine my attitude toward other believers. Do I have the attitude that since we don't agree on every issue, other believers are not my brothers and sisters and I shouldn't have anything to do with them? Or do I approach fellow Christians with a loving heart and try to identify the ways in which we can work together for the common good? In short, do I have an attitude of confrontation or one of acceptance?

Over the past year and a half, I have been amazed at the publicity that the Mayberry Bible study concept has received. When you stop and think about it, it's really a very simple approach. You examine a show in which people can identify with the characters and situations presented. Then you reflect on those stories and think about how God can work in those same situations in your own life. In a nutshell, that's about it. People have really taken an interest in this concept, and it's not limited to a particular church or denomination. Baptists, Methodists, Catholics, Presbyterians, Churches of Christ, and others have all started Mayberry classes of their own. The simple messages of Mayberry seems to have transcended denominational boundaries. When you try to pinpoint the commonality, I believe it comes down to the fact that we all have the same ideals and goals, which include living a family-oriented, moral lifestyle in the service of our Lord. My ongoing hope is that this concept as well as others will continue to bring us closer together.

CHAPTER 18

HAPPINESS IS A CHOICE

"The Christmas Story"

Suddenly a great company of the heavenly host appeared with the angel, praising God and saying, "Glory to God in the highest, and on earth peace to men on whom his favor rests."

Luke 2:13–14

In the eight-year run of *The Andy Griffith Show*, there was only one Christmas episode. "The Christmas Story" came early in the series, as it was the eleventh episode of the first season. The episode follows the theme of a traditional Dickens *Christmas Carol*, but with a Mayberry spin. Barney and Andy are in the courthouse on Christmas Eve opening Christmas cards and enjoying the spirit of the season. Andy is discussing all the plans that he and Aunt Bee have made to celebrate Christmas, and the conversation drifts to who will play Santa Claus this year. Barney initially volunteers, but he remembers he has guard duty since the Mayberry jail is uncharacteristically full. Andy will not hear of Barney having to spend Christmas Eve at the courthouse, so he joyfully

dismisses all the prisoners with the promise that they will return just as soon as Christmas is over. The local prisoners are
grateful to Andy, and all agree to return in a couple of days.
Everything is in place for Andy and his family and friends to
have a wonderful Christmas celebration at home.

That is, until Ben Weaver enters the courthouse dragging
Sam Muggins behind him. If you remember, Ben Weaver is
the crusty old gent who runs Weaver's Department Store, the
only department store in Mayberry. It seems that Ben has
caught Sam moonshining. You may ask, Why would Ben
care if Sam was moonshining? Several episodes indicate that
the town of Mayberry is in a dry county and the sale of any
alcoholic beverages is prohibited. However, in this episode
Ben can legally sell spirits at his store, and he is angry that
Sam is making his own brands. Ben's complaint is that Sam
is illegally cutting in on his business.

Andy can't believe Ben is serious. While Sam's actions are
illegal, Andy knows that Ben's complaint is ridiculous. Andy
tries to smooth things over, but Ben insists that Sam be
locked up. Andy realizes that he is getting nowhere with
Ben, so he does the only thing he can do; he puts Sam in a
cell. Sam, who has obviously been caught off guard by the
whole situation, wonders aloud how his wife and two young
children will get along without him at Christmastime. Ben
angrily reminds Sam that if he hadn't been breaking the law,
he wouldn't be in this situation in the first place.

Andy appears to be in a bit of a predicament. Earlier he
was able to release his prisoners so they could go home and
be with their families. That action also freed up Barney to
celebrate with Andy's family. Now, not only did Andy have
another prisoner on his hands, but Sam's family was at home

alone without their father. At this point Andy could have re-
acted in several ways. First, he could have had the attitude
of Ben Weaver and just dismissed Sam as being in a situation
that he created himself. After all, it was his own fault. Andy
could have just gone home and left Sam and Barney at the
jail without another thought. Or, Andy could have fretted
and worried about what to do. He could have complained
about how his plans were ruined and about how unfair life
was to him. He could have made everyone around him miserable because he wasn't getting his way.

Andy took a different approach. Instead of focusing on
his own interests or complaining about how he was being
inconvenienced, Andy devised a plan to meet everyone's
needs. First, Andy went out and "arrested" Sam's family as
being accessories to the crime. Then, after he brought Sam's
wife, Bess, his daughter, Effie, and his son, Billy, to the courthouse, Andy called Aunt Bee and Miss Ellie to tell them that
Christmas was going to be at the courthouse this year.
Everyone pitched in to help. Barney went out and got a
Christmas tree, while Aunt Bee and Miss Ellie brought all the
food and trimmings. The courthouse was transformed from
a cold prison into a warm and loving home. As a side note,
Andy Griffith and Eleanor Donahue (Miss Ellie) performed a
beautiful rendition of "Away in a Manger" as the festivities
continued at the courthouse.

The only person not pleased by all this was, and you
guessed it, Ben Weaver. At every step, Ben tries to thwart
Andy's plan to bring Christmas to the courthouse, but Andy
will not be denied. After a while, Ben begins to act peculiar.
He begins to commit some petty crimes for no apparent reason. In one instance, Ben attempts to steal a public bench

from just outside the courthouse. Andy considers arresting him, but Miss Ellie reminds Andy that it is Christmas, and Andy lets him go. Then Barney runs Ben in for parking in front of a fire hydrant, but again Ben's violation is forgiven. Eventually Andy realizes what is going on. Ben is lonely, but he is too proud to admit it. He is trying his best to get arrested so that he can be included in the celebration. Finally

Andy does "arrest" Ben and allows him to go back home to get a few things since he will be spending the night in jail. However, when they arrive back at the courthouse, we find that Ben has filled his suitcase full of gifts for everyone. Even though he is still reluctant to admit it, Ben has finally come to appreciate the true meaning of Christmas.

This episode teaches me that no matter what my situation, the choice to be happy (or not) is mine to make. I can find bad in any situation, and if I choose to focus on the negative, I will probably be unhappy. I think Ben Weaver's problem was that he felt sorry for himself, and instead of trying to do something about it, he chose to make everybody around him as miserable as he was. Andy, on the other hand, had his problems too. I'm sure he didn't originally plan to spend Christmas at the courthouse, but that did not affect his attitude or spirit. No matter what happened, he maintained a positive attitude and was constantly concerned with the needs of the others. It makes you wonder if that selfless attitude of putting others before yourself might be a key to true happiness.

The Christmas of 1998 was definitely one to remember in our family's household. Nicole and I had planned to drive to McMinnville, Tennessee, on Christmas Eve to be with my dad's side of the family. After a traditional Christmas dinner with my grandmother, we would then drive the short trip back to Tullahoma where my parents lived. The day before Christmas Eve, we were uncharacteristically ready to go early. All the shopping had been done, and we were packed and ready to leave first thing the next morning. Then it started.

We don't get much snow in North Alabama, but we have some really nasty ice storms, and this one was coming fast.

We hadn't planned to leave on the twenty-third, but since the roads were worsening, we decided to go ahead and drive to my parents' house. That way, if the roads did get bad during the night, we wouldn't have to worry about making the trip the next morning. We got to my parents' house fine, but the ice storm continued. At about 5:30 P.M., the power went out, and it soon became obvious that it wasn't coming back on anytime soon. By the time we went to bed, the house had cooled considerably. None of us got much sleep that night because of all the trees and limbs crashing to the ground due to the weight of the ice. The next morning, Christmas Eve, it was downright cold in the house, but the good news was that my grandmother's power was on. The forty-five-mile drive from Tullahoma to McMinnville was like driving through a war zone. Trees were literally everywhere, and so were power lines. By early that morning, the lines at the service stations to buy kerosene were long and getting longer.

After a nice (warm) visit at my grandmother's house, we made the trek back to Tullahoma. The house was still dark, and the temperature inside was in the mid-thirties. This was worse than camping. The next day was Christmas, but nobody seemed to care. We were cold and miserable.

That Christmas morning was unlike any other Christmas morning we had experienced. There was no power to light the tree. It was so cold in the house that the houseplants were starting to die, and we certainly couldn't have a traditional Christmas breakfast. All that didn't stop my mom from trying. She had cut up some fruit before we woke up. Then she heated water using the gas grill so at least we could have hot coffee and oatmeal. Let me tell you, when you're sitting in the dark, freezing, and eating oatmeal on

Christmas morning, it is easy to start feeling sorry for your-self. So I did. But the situation caused me to think about some things that I would not have thought about if every-thing had been perfect. I began to think about what it would be like if I lived this way all the time and didn't have the everyday luxuries I constantly take for granted. What if I had to worry about where I would sleep every night and whether it would be warm or not? What if I had to worry about what I would eat, or if I would have anything to eat at all?

I also thought about how I tend to rely on external things to make me happy. As long as I have a good job and a nice house, then I'll be happy. When everything in my life works out the way I want it to, then I'll be happy. Then I began to realize the danger in this thinking. If I base my happiness solely on external factors, things I can't control, how can I ever truly be happy? No matter how well we plan our lives, some things are not going to work out the way we want them to. Things will go wrong, and it is up to us to decide how we will react to those disasters we all experience.

Andy had his Christmas plans turned upside down at the last minute, but that didn't dampen his Christmas spirit one bit. In fact, he and others may have had the best Christmas of all because they were finally able to touch the heart of mean old Ben Weaver—all because everyone decided to pitch in and make the best of what they were given. When the events in our lives don't go exactly according to plan, will we wallow in our misery or will we look for the good in the situation? After all, when it comes to our happiness, it really is a choice.

THE PRICE OF VICTORY

"A Medal for Opie"

*Brothers, I do not consider myself yet to have taken hold
of it. But one thing I do: Forgetting what is behind and
straining toward what is ahead, I press on toward the goal
to win the prize for which God has called me heavenward
in Christ Jesus.*

Philippians 3:13–14

Have you ever bargained with God? In other words, have
you ever promised God you will do something if He will just
give you what you want or get you out of a jam? I think all
of us have done this at one time or another. It's a part of our
human nature. In the episode "A Medal for Opie" Opie
makes a bargain with God. If God will let him win a first-
place medal at the Sheriff's Boys' Day track meet, then Opie
will take it off when he takes a bath every once in a while.
Winning the 50-yard dash means everything to Opie. He
even dreams about winning the race and taking home the
prize. Opie is no slouch in preparing for the race either.
Under the coaching of Barney, Opie jogs and jumps rope to

build up his strength. The big day finally comes, and Opie ends up finishing last.

Opie can't believe it. He is crushed. All the training, hard work, and preparation, and he finishes last. Opie leaves the track in disgust. He doesn't congratulate his fellow competitors. He doesn't even say good-bye. He just leaves. Later Andy tries to explain to his son the importance of being a good loser, but Opie rejects Andy's advice. Opie prefers to wallow in his misery. Andy tells his son how disappointed he is in his attitude, but for now Opie is content to be a sore loser.

As this episode shows us, we learn about winning and losing at a very early age. When I think about my own experiences as a youngster, I remember wanting to emulate the people I perceived as being winners, people who were dedicated and had the respect of their peers. Those were the people I wanted to be like, and one of those people made an impression on me at an early age. The first time I saw him in real life was on September 29, 1979, at Vanderbilt Stadium in Nashville, Tennessee. He was on the sidelines before the game with a program rolled up in one hand and that famous houndstooth hat perched on his head. It was really him. For a boy of thirteen, it was quite a thrill to see him, even from a distance. His expression matched his worn, tough face as he watched his players warm up amid the flashes of the news reporters' cameras. That day, Paul "Bear" Bryant led his Alabama team to victory against Vanderbilt by a score of 66–3 and would eventually go on to win the national championship that year. Not much of a game for the spectators that day, but that didn't matter to this young Alabama fan. I actually got to see him. I got to see "The Bear" in person.

To date, Paul W. Bryant is the winningest coach of Division I college football. His 324 wins were accumulated at the University of Kentucky, Texas A&M, and the University of Alabama. Bryant always joked that he would "croak in a week" if he ever gave up coaching football. Ironically, within a month of his final game against Illinois in the 1982 Liberty Bowl, Paul W. Bryant died. Bryant had no secret or special formula for success when he coached, but he coached his players for success in football and also for success in life. In Bryant's words, "Sacrifice. Work. Self-discipline. I teach these things, and my boys don't forget them when they leave." In one of the more memorable, if not infamous, events during his coaching career, Bryant took 111 Texas A&M football players to a place called Junction, Texas, for a ten-day football camp before the 1954 season. By the end of the ten days, only thirty-five were left. The rest had quit the team because of Bryant's brutal schedule and the horrible desert conditions in the drought-ridden town of Junction. The few who survived went on to great success both on and off the field.

One of the Junction survivors was Gene Stallings. You would probably think that an experience like Junction would be something that one would like to forget, but Stallings has repeatedly said that the experience molded his character and forged his winning spirit. And that character and winning spirit would be evident in Stallings' career as a coach himself. Stallings returned to his alma mater in 1965 and coached for seven years. Then he spent fourteen years as an assistant to Tom Landry with the Dallas Cowboys. After a brief time as head coach with the Phoenix Cardinals, Gene Stallings followed his mentor's footsteps and returned to Alabama as the head coach in 1990.

Success didn't come immediately for Stallings at
Alabama. In fact, he lost his first three games as the
Crimson Tide's head coach. Many people at the time
thought that Stallings was the wrong coach to replace Bill
Curry, who had recently departed for Kentucky. Some said
that he wasn't a motivator. Others said that his coaching
practices were out of style and no longer valid in today's
game. After getting off to a rocky start, Stallings persisted,
and the wins began to come. What began as a disastrous
season actually ended respectably with a record of 7–5. The
next year under Stallings, Alabama finished a quiet 11–1.
Then in 1992, the Alabama football team won its twelfth
national championship under head coach Gene Stallings by
defeating the University of Miami in the Sugar Bowl.

For every success we achieve there will be many failures.
I'm sure that when Gene Stallings was 0–3 in his first season
at Alabama he didn't have many reasons to hold his head up
and be confident, and I'm sure he had moments when he felt
like quitting. But I imagine that during those tough times,
Stallings remembered a few things his old coach had once
said, "The first time you quit, it's hard. The second time, it
gets easier. The third time, you don't even have to think
about it." Just because we prepare for events in our lives
doesn't guarantee that we will always come in first. We
should expect hard times and failures along the way, but
they shouldn't defeat us. We shouldn't let them keep us
down. If we can learn from our losses instead of being consumed by them, then I believe the road to our championship
will be a little easier.

In the end, Opie has a change of heart. The hurt of losing is still there, but he begins to realize his responsibility to

handle losing as well as winning. But more important to Opie is the fact that he doesn't want to be a disappointment in the eyes of his father. He wants his pa to always be proud of him. In a touching scene, Opie apologizes to Andy for his behavior and asks for his forgiveness. Andy is proud that Opie has learned an important lesson about life. He reminds his son that he doesn't have to be happy about losing, but he should be prepared to accept it. After all, winning and losing are a part of life.

If you believe in yourself and have dedication and pride—and never quit—you'll be a winner. The price of victory is high, but so are the rewards.

Paul W. Bryant

CHAPTER 20
CHANGES

"The New Housekeeper"

Praise be to the God and Father of our Lord Jesus Christ, the Father of compassion and the God of all comfort, who comforts us in all our troubles, so that we can comfort those in any trouble with the comfort we ourselves have received from God.

2 Corinthians 1:3–4

I can identify with Opie in the episode "The New Housekeeper" because neither of us like change. Opie's current housekeeper and mother figure, Rose, is getting married. Although we are not given the details, we can assume that Rose is the only mother Opie has ever known, and now she is leaving Opie for some guy named Wilbur. Opie is obviously unhappy about the marriage and does everything he can to disrupt the ceremony at the courthouse. Finally, Barney has to cover Opie's mouth so that Andy, the justice of the peace, can finish the ceremony. After Rose is gone, Opie strongly opposes the idea of a new housekeeper. He even tries to make breakfast for Andy the next morning to show him that he can do all the things that Rose used to do. Unfortunately for Opie, this does not change Andy's mind, and the new housekeeper arrives.

As you may have guessed, the new housekeeper is none other than Aunt Bee. Those of you not as familiar with the series may not have known that Aunt Bee's arrival was initially met with much resistance from Opie. Aunt Bee was such an intricate part of the Mayberry family that we forget she almost didn't make it! When Aunt Bee arrives at the Taylor household, Opie immediately rejects her. After all, she can't fish, hunt frogs, or play baseball like Rose did. Aunt Bee tries her best to do all the things that Opie wants, but it soon becomes evident that she is just not much of an angler or an athlete. Andy tries to help the situation by reminding Opie that Aunt Bee did a wonderful job of raising Andy himself as a child. Andy asks Opie to try to put Rose out of his mind and give Aunt Bee a chance.

This is a tough situation for a little boy. Basically, his whole world has been turned upside down. Not only is he dealing with the hurt of Rose leaving, but he is being forced to accept Aunt Bee, who by his standards can't do anything. He wants things to be like they were, not like they are now. Is this any different from my attitude when things in my life change? Probably not. Several things go through our minds when change comes in our lives. First of all, we are fearful of the unknown. Our carefully laid pieces have been disturbed, and we're not quite sure how they are going to be put back together again. That is, we're not sure how everything is going to work out, and that makes us uncomfortable.

I remember a time in my life, when I was not much older than Opie, that a fairly major disruption occurred in my small world. I was about ten years old and had gotten pretty used to the way things were. In addition to my mom and dad, I had an older sister, Gwen, who was thirteen, and a younger brother, David, who was six. Even though I was physically bigger than my sister, I still had that same respect for her that a younger dog has for an older one. You know, even though the younger dog might be much larger and stronger, he still doesn't mess with the older dog. No matter how big you get, you always remember who came first. But even though Gwen was the boss of us kids, I still had power over David. After all, I was ten, and he was only six. So life continued as normal until a particular family trip to the beach. Then the apple cart of my life was suddenly turned over when my mom told us that our threesome was going to become a foursome.

Why in the world would they want another one? I thought. I would have told them that three was enough, but they obviously didn't ask me. Well, this was definitely going to change things. Gone was the normal life that we had become accustomed to. The focus would now be on someone new. At this point, I think I could relate to how Opie felt in the episode. I'm a little angry that this new person is coming into my life, but I'm more scared because I'm not sure how it's all going to work out. *How will this new person affect me; how will the person affect my relationship with my mom and dad? Will they have any time left for me? Why couldn't they have just left things the way they were?* All worrisome questions for a ten-year-old.

Back to the episode. Aunt Bee, feeling that Opie will never accept her, reluctantly decides to leave. Andy asks Aunt Bee to give it a little more time, but she is determined. The next morning, Aunt Bee and Andy are up and ready to leave for the bus station, but before they can go Opie runs out to stop them. Andy and Aunt Bee are both surprised at Opie's sudden change of attitude, but they soon understand.

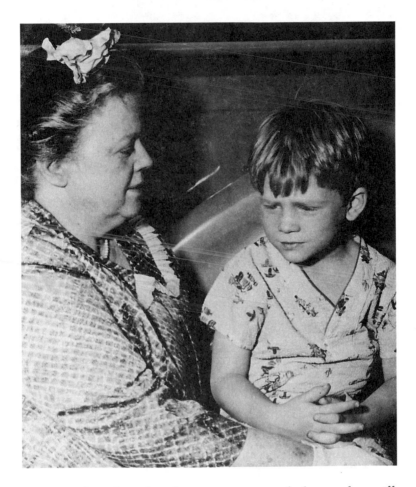

It seems that Opie has become concerned about what will happen to Aunt Bee if she can't even perform the basic activities of life, such as fishing and hunting frogs. He sees it as his duty to teach Aunt Bee these things, since there is obviously no one else to do it. In other words, Aunt Bee must stay because she needs Opie.

The relationship is now set for the entire series. Andy, Aunt Bee, and Opie are a family; they all need and serve one another. Opie was willing to forgo his needs because he perceived the needs of another to be greater than his own. When he took the responsibility for taking care of Aunt Bee, concerns about his wants seemed to pale in comparison.

On January 7, 1977, my second little brother, Michael, made it to this earth. I immediately determined that he needed me. After all, who was better qualified to teach him about creeks, rocks, snakes, and the other important things in a boy's life than me? At that point I wasn't concerned about the way things used to be or the fact that my life was going to be quite different from now on. I was more concerned about my responsibility of raising him the way a ten-year-old big brother should. Looking back over the past twenty-two years, it is easy to see how a change I was initially afraid of turned out to be such a blessing. At the time, however, the thought of change was uncomfortable. To this day, I am still resistant to change. I tend to like things the way they are, and I become upset when someone starts messing with my ducks when I have them neatly in a row. However, when I stop and think about the opportunities and blessings that so often accompany change, I can't help but be excited about the possibilities.

CHAPTER 21

SHE'S NICE, SHE'S REAL NICE!

"A Date for Gomer"

Therefore, as God's chosen people, holy and dearly loved, clothe yourselves with compassion, kindness, humility, gentleness and patience. Bear with each other and forgive whatever grievances you may have against one another. Forgive as the Lord forgave you. And over all these virtues put on love, which binds them all together in perfect unity.

Colossians 3:12–14

It seems that Andy and Barney have a problem. It's only a couple of days until the big Chamber of Commerce dance, and Thelma Lou's cousin, Mary Grace, has come to visit for a few days. The problem is that Thelma Lou will not go to the dance with Barney unless they can set up a date for Mary Grace as well. At first Barney protests. It would be impossible to find a date for Mary Grace, he says, because she's a dog. Thelma Lou can't believe Barney would be so cruel to speak of her cousin in such a way, and she threatens never to speak to Barney again. Barney can't believe that

121

his big plans for the dance are about to be dashed because of Mary Grace. Desperate, Barney solicits Andy's help to find a date for Mary Grace. Both Barney and Andy agree that the prospective person should be a little naïve, or "knave" as Barney would say. While they are discussing prospective candidates, Gomer Pyle happens to walk into the courthouse.

Barney and Andy approach Gomer about taking Mary Grace to the big dance. Gomer is interested, but when he asks what she looks like, Barney and Andy change the subject by saying, "She's nice." They are obviously concerned that if Gomer knows what Mary Grace looks like, he won't agree to take her. Finally, Gomer agrees to take Mary Grace and the plans are set. However, Andy warns Gomer not to "over expect." On the night of the dance, Barney, Andy, and Gomer arrive at Thelma Lou's house to pick up the girls, including Andy's date, Helen Crump. Shortly after they arrive, Gomer excuses himself by saying that he has forgotten to do something. Thelma Lou and Helen are outraged. They can't believe Gomer would be so rude as to leave five minutes after arriving. Mary Grace tells Thelma Lou and Helen to go on to the dance with Andy and Barney. The girls hesitate at first but finally agree to go. When they arrive at the dance, Thelma Lou is so mad that she refuses to get out of the car. The thought of standing in a stag line with a bunch of slumped over teenagers doesn't appeal to Barney, so the foursome head back home.

Meanwhile, there is a knock at the door back at Thelma Lou's house. Mary Grace answers and it is Gomer holding a corsage. Earlier, Gomer noticed that Thelma Lou and Helen had corsages, but Mary Grace did not. He thought it would be a shame for Mary Grace to go to the dance unadorned. Gomer apologizes for taking so long, but he had to go to two stores to find one with pink in it to match Mary Grace's dress. Mary Grace can't believe that Gomer would go to so much trouble just for her. Barney, Andy, Helen, and Thelma Lou return to the house to find Gomer and Mary Grace

having a great time dancing to records. Without missing a beat, Gomer comments to Andy that he was right all along. Mary Grace is nice. She's real nice!

While "A Date for Gomer" is an extremely funny episode, it has some serious undertones about how we treat one another. When Barney hears that Thelma Lou wants to find a date for Mary Grace, he immediately discounts the idea because, in his words, "Mary Grace is a dog." Even for Barney, that assessment is pretty cruel: no mention of her personality or inner qualities, just a cheap shot at her appearance. Unfortunately, Andy's behavior isn't much better. He assumes that he will have to mislead Gomer in order to get him to commit to the dance. In an attempt to change the subject away from her appearance, Andy calls Mary Grace "nice." This is obviously a statement to divert the conversation, but an attribute Gomer takes seriously. Gomer is the only one willing to give Mary Grace a chance.

As genuine as Gomer is, it doesn't take much for the others to lose faith in him. When Gomer abruptly leaves the house soon after they arrive, everyone assumes that he has bolted because he doesn't think Mary Grace is pretty enough. But Gomer has a good heart. He isn't concerned about looks or having fun at the dance. He is concerned about Mary Grace. He wants the best for her, even if it requires a little extra effort. Gomer takes the time to look past the physical and see the person, and when he makes the effort to do that, he finds a person that Barney and Andy completely missed. Gomer finds Mary Grace to be really nice, and that is the real truth!

To look at her, you wouldn't have thought that Anna amounted to much. She wasn't dressed very nicely, and she was a bit overweight. She obviously didn't have much money, or she wouldn't have been at the church to pick up food for her family. By most people's standards, she was a nobody, a tax on the welfare system, part of the problem, someone to be dismissed and ignored. What a shame it would be if people judged Anna solely on her physical appearance.

Just saying hello to her made you feel good. She had the brightest smile and the friendliest attitude. We started talking and I found out that she was the mother of two young children and had taken in another teenager because his mother would have nothing to do with him. Anna couldn't stand the thought of him growing up without anyone who cared. Anna's husband had recently left her because he couldn't handle the pressure of the new kid in the household. It seemed that when the boy first came to live with them, he had some major behavioral problems and was a load to handle. Anna didn't want her husband to leave, but she would not turn the boy out either. She decided to keep the boy in their house and hopes that one day she and her husband will work things out.

With all of this going on, Anna is making a living by taking care of an elderly lady in the first stages of Alzheimer's disease. It is a challenging and thankless job, but in her heart she knows that there is good in what she is doing. You see, Anna wants to go back to school one day and become a doctor. As another way to bring in money, she works part-time in a doctor's office to get some hands-on experience dealing with people, as if she needs it. After talking with her for just fifteen minutes, I realized that she is one of the most selfless, caring individuals I have ever met. During the whole conversation, she never mentioned her own needs. She didn't complain about how bad things were or how she had been handed a raw deal in life. Her only concern was for those around her.

Another thing that really impressed me was Anna's patience and faith. She has gone through a lot in this life, but she seems content to wait on God. She knows she has problems. She knows that money is tight and the kids need food and clothing. She is still trying to repair her marriage. But she is at peace. She knows that God is going to work things out in His time, not hers, and she has the patience to wait on Him. I compare the physical blessings in my life with those of hers and wonder how I ever have the gall to complain. Compared to Anna, I have so much; yet my attitude of humility and selflessness doesn't come close to hers. She faces daily challenges I have never had to face, but she is content. She knows who is in control, and she knows that she will be taken care of.

Even though we met just once, Anna is still a great inspiration to me. She gave me the encouragement and perspective I needed that day. And to think, I presumptuously thought that I would be the one encouraging her. This experience, along with this Mayberry episode, causes me to think about my attitude toward others. Do I automatically judge others by what they look like? If so, how many people like Anna have I missed getting to know? Above all else, this experience teaches me the blessings of getting to know the heart of a person. Anna was a special person, someone I will never forget. Whether or not she eventually becomes a doctor, she has already proven to be a great success to the ones whose lives she has touched.

CHAPTER 22

CENTER OF ATTENTION

"Barney and the Choir"

Pride goes before destruction, a haughty spirit before a
fall.

Proverbs 16:18

The Mayberry choir is in trouble. The lead tenor, Ralph Pritchard, has just dropped out because of a work conflict. This couldn't have come at a worse time for the choir director, John Masters. It is less than two weeks until the next concert, and the choir must perform well if they have any chance to be invited to the state finals. John knows he must find a new tenor and find one fast, but he has no prospective candidates. He goes to the courthouse to solicit Andy's help.

When John arrives at Andy's office, he finds Andy, Barney, and Aunt Bee there. After relaying the dreadful news, Andy and Aunt Bee suggest other candidates to fill the void left by Ralph Pritchard, but no one is identified. During the conversation, you can see the wheels in Barney's head spinning. Barney knows who should be the next lead tenor in the

Mayberry choir. Why, the obvious choice would be none other than Barney Fife! A confident Barney drops a hint to John Masters that he has taken voice lessons, a hint that he has to repeat three times before John picks up on it. Finally, John asks Barney to join the choir. Barney enthusiastically agrees, but Andy and Aunt Bee aren't so sure. You see, before John Masters arrived at the courthouse, Barney was giving a little concert of his own, and it was painfully obvious that the only person who could appreciate his ability to sing was Barney himself!

Later on that evening, the choir meets to practice for the upcoming concert. Barney is excited to be there and takes center stage. However, when the choir begins the first number, John Masters immediately recognizes that something is wrong. He thinks he hears a sour note. John begins the song again, and the result is the same. Someone in the choir is definitely singing off key. At this point Barney jumps down from the stage and whispers to John that he will move around during the singing of the song to see if he can determine who is singing off key. John agrees that this is a good idea, and they start the song one more time. Barney begins moving around the group, and one by one the choir members stop singing when they realize how bad Barney sounds. Eventually, the only one left singing is Barney, and he really does sound terrible! Completely oblivious to the whole situation, Barney whispers to John that he didn't have time to spot the guilty party because John cut him off too soon. It never occurs to Barney that he might be the one singing off key.

The episode, "Barney and the Choir," is yet another example of our favorite deputy putting himself in the limelight. From the beginning of the episode, it is obvious that Barney has no talent for singing. Even his loving girlfriend, Thelma Lou, states that he can't sing a lick. But that doesn't stop Barney. His desire to be the center of attention gets the best of him. You would think that eventually Barney would learn from his own mistakes, that he would realize that the world doesn't always revolve around him. But time and time again, Barney manages to get himself in a mess. In his efforts to prove himself and to showcase his own abilities, Barney usually ends up needing a helping hand. Fortunately, Barney has a friend like Andy who is always willing to bail him out.

When reflecting on Barney and his desire to promote himself, I can't help but think of the apostle Peter. Peter was also constantly trying to prove himself, but on many occasions he failed. The night that Jesus walked on the water, Peter was eager to prove his faith by walking out to meet the Lord. However, when it actually came down to stepping out of the boat, his faith weakened and he began to sink. Peter boasted that he would always be there to defend Jesus, that he would be the one who would never let Him down. But on the night of the crucifixion, Peter denied his friend three times. Even after Jesus' death, Peter initially did not believe the first reports of the resurrection even though Jesus had told him that it would happen.

In his quest to be the most faithful follower of Jesus, Peter often missed the boat. His shortcomings seemed to surface when he focused on himself and not on the Lord. You would think that the man who was that close to Jesus, who walked with Him and heard His teachings, who witnessed many of His miracles, would never have a problem keeping his priorities straight. You would think that a man in Peter's position would never struggle with the issues of pride, self-reliance, and humility. However, Peter was human and he made mistakes. This realization gives me hope and encouragement as I face the daily struggles in my own life.

I would venture to say that Barney Fife is, without a doubt, the most popular character in Mayberry. And I believe that one reason for this is because we can all see a little bit of ourselves in Barney. We can understand his desire to be popular and accepted by others, and we can identify with his tendency to focus on himself and to have an over-confident attitude. However, I also believe we can learn something from Barney. That is, when we do have the attitude that we ourselves are sufficient, chances are we will come up short. As I mentioned before, Barney was fortunate to have a friend like Andy to help him out of the situations he got himself into. We are fortunate as well. Like Peter, we have the greatest friend possible who understands what it's like to be human and knows all the trials and temptations we face. A friend who is patient and quick to forgive. A friend who will help us out of any mess we get ourselves into. Isn't it wonderful that we have this kind of friend in Jesus!

CHAPTER 23

ROBIN HOOD

"Opie and His Merry Men"

But godliness with contentment is great gain. For we brought nothing into the world, and we can take nothing out of it. But if we have food and clothing, we will be content with that. People who want to get rich fall into temptation and a trap and into many foolish and harmful desires that plunge men into ruin and destruction. For the love of money is a root of all kinds of evil. Some people, eager for money, have wandered from the faith and pierced themselves with many griefs.

1 Timothy 6:6–10

"Are any of you boys rich?" the hobo asks Opie and his friends. The reaction the boys give is a little odd. In fact, none of the four boys have an answer. There are no positive or negative responses. They shrug their shoulders and say they don't know. They don't know if they are rich or not.

That was a very small scene in the episode "Opie and His Merry Men" but I thought it was interesting. At this point in the series, Opie and his friends seem to be around twelve years old. They have been running around in the woods playing "Robin Hood" when they come across Willie, a hobo who has set up camp nearby. It seems that Willie is down on his luck because of all the injustice that life has dealt him. He can't work because he has a bad leg from saving the life of a baby who was about to be run over by a train. Willie convinces the boys that it is their duty as disciples of Robin Hood to steal from the rich and give to the poor, and of course, Willie is poor. The boys are happy to oblige Willie by giving him things they take from home, but soon the boys' parents begin to notice the missing items.

Opie is a little confused by the whole situation. He asks why some people have everything they need while others have nothing. He just doesn't think it's fair that some people have to struggle just to make ends meet. When Andy finds out what the boys are doing, he reminds them that stealing is stealing and what they are doing is wrong, regardless of their good intentions. Opie asks Andy how it can be wrong if Willie can't help himself. Andy takes this opportunity to show the boys that Willie isn't quite as helpless as he claims to be. When Andy offers Willie a job and a place to stay, the hobo hightails it out of there, bad leg and all. It's now obvious that Willie is a freeloader, a lesson not lost on Opie and his friends.

During the episode, Opie asks Andy and Aunt Bee if they are rich. At first Andy says no, that you can't get rich on a sheriff's salary. Barney pipes in by saying that if you do, you're sure to be investigated! After Andy thinks for a minute, he dismisses their material wealth and remembers the other things. Andy tells Opie that their basic needs are being met, such as having a roof over their heads and plenty of food to eat. He mentions family and the fact that Andy, Opie, and Aunt Bee have each other. He also mentions that they are blessed with good friends like Barney. Andy begins to realize how much they do have to be thankful for and that, yes, they are indeed rich.

This scene reminded me of an experience I had as a young boy. I remember one night when I was about twelve years old, my teammates and I had just finished playing a Little League baseball game. We had won the game, and one of the fathers had taken the whole team out for ice cream. Best I remember, wins for our team came few and far between, so we definitely had cause for celebration. However, what I remember most about that night occurred when one of the coaches brought me home. Our family had recently moved into the house my dad and grandfather built. It was a two-story house located just outside of the city on about fifteen acres of land. As we approached the house, the coach took one look and said, "Oh, so here's where the rich people live." At the time I really didn't pay attention to what he said, but the more I thought about it, the more it bothered me. Was I rich? I didn't think I was rich. Growing up in a single-income family with four kids doesn't really give you the feeling of expendable wealth. But this guy obviously thought by the house we lived in that we must be rich.

Of course, he didn't know that my dad and grandfather had done all the subcontracting and a lot of the work themselves. I'm sure my dad was able to build that house for about half of what it would have cost if we had tried to buy it from a builder, but I didn't understand all that back then. I was more concerned with the question of being rich and what that really meant. Upon further reflection, I decided that I must be rich. For starters, I had my own room. That was a definite improvement over our situation in the other house where my brother David and I had to share a room that was about half the size of a master bedroom closet in today's homes. Another thing that was high on a twelve-year-old's mind was food. We rarely ate out, but we always seemed to have enough to eat, so we obviously weren't poor. As far as clothes went, I really didn't notice that most of my clothes came from Hammer's, a local discount store. In fact, some of my favorite shoes were hand-me-downs. We had two cars, so I guess you could count us as rich. One car was a late-seventies station wagon that got about the same gas mileage as an armored personnel carrier, and the other car was an Astre, the Pontiac version of the Vega. For those of you who remember the Vega, you can guess how much luck I had getting dates when I began driving a few years later. But everything considered, I concluded that we were indeed rich.

That feeling soon began to change. As I approached my teenage years, I begin to rethink my assessment of our wealth. As my friends and I turned sixteen, several of them received cars of their own. Nice cars. Firebirds, Sunbirds, and other hot models of the early eighties. I also had a Pontiac, but it didn't have "bird" in the name. The Astre was a 1976 model complete with peeling paint and a leaking windshield. To make matters worse, I didn't have sole possession of the car. I shared it with my parents and my older sister. At that point in my life, I was a little more conscious of my clothes as well. Suddenly, the outfits from Hammer's didn't seem so cool. But, money was tight and nice clothes were a little hard to come by. By this time, I was absolutely, positively sure that we were not rich.

After college, things changed again. I was fortunate enough to find a good job. For the first time in my life, I had money. I was able to buy a car and eventually a house, and then a bigger house. I bought nice clothes, and I was able to eat out whenever I wanted. I had made it. I had arrived. I was rich.

As the years go by, the material things mean less and less to me. I realize how easy it is to get caught up in the materialistic rat race our society promotes. Things that used to be very important to me no longer are. Furthermore, the things I didn't consider as important, or didn't notice at the time, are very important to me now. When I was twelve and was trying to determine if I was rich, I never considered the fact that I lived with both my parents. I never counted the fact that I had four grandparents who took an active role in my life. I surely didn't count the fact that I had an older sister and two younger brothers around. However, when I look back on my childhood, those are the things I cherish. Those are the people who made me rich.

It's easy to go through life and to think about the material things you don't have. And if you constantly focus on all the things you have yet to acquire, you will probably never consider yourself as being rich. However, if you stop and seriously consider the true blessings in your life, the things that you wouldn't take any amount of money in exchange for, you begin to realize how rich you really are. When Opie asked Andy if they were rich, his immediate reaction was no. For most of us, that would probably be our initial reaction as well. But as he began to reflect, Andy realized just how much they had to be thankful for. When I take the time to count my own blessings, I am amazed by how rich I really am.

CHAPTER 24

FIRST LAW OF FRIENDSHIP

"The Case of the Punch in the Nose"

We who are strong ought to bear with the failings of the weak and not to please ourselves. Each of us should please his neighbor for his good, to build him up.

Accept one another, then, just as Christ accepted you, in order to bring praise to God.

Romans 15:1–2, 7

As Americans, few things upset us more than feeling that our rights have been violated. In this day and age, we value our personal rights. We have a long and proud history of defending and preserving our freedom and our right to life, liberty, and the pursuit of happiness. I am not knocking this great heritage, but I wonder if it is possible to take the attitude of personal rights too far. Can we be so consumed with ourselves and our rights that we become blind to everything else around us?

In the episode "The Case of the Punch in the Nose" Andy and Barney are going through some old files at the courthouse. As they often do, Andy and Barney are humming an old spiritual as they pass the time away. "Sinners Lose All Their Guilty Stains," Andy reminds Barney after he questions the name of the song. As they continue their work, Barney comes across a file, an assault case between Floyd the barber and Charlie Foley, who runs the local grocery. Andy and Barney can't believe that two men as gentle as Floyd and Mr. Foley would actually be involved in an assault case, but it's all there in black and white—all there except for how the case was resolved. Barney is immediately curious and states that it is their duty as law officers to investigate since the principles in the case are still living in Mayberry. Andy reminds Barney that the case is almost twenty years old, and he doesn't see the wisdom in reopening a case that happened so long ago.

As you can imagine, Barney will not be denied. He marches down to the barbershop to get the story from Floyd. Floyd, however, is much more concerned with an article in today's newspaper than he is about an incident that happened twenty years ago. After Barney is unsuccessful at getting any information from Floyd, he visits Mr. Foley down at the market. Mr. Foley fondly remembers the story. It seems that Floyd and Mr. Foley had gotten into an argument over the price of a shave. One thing led to another, and Mr. Foley claims that Floyd punched him in the nose. Mr. Foley has a good laugh remembering the story, but Barney doesn't see the humor. Back at the barbershop, Floyd's memory makes a dramatic recovery upon hearing Foley's account of the story. Floyd now claims that it was Foley who had done the punching.

A few minutes later, Mr. Foley and Goober arrive at the barbershop. Floyd and Mr. Foley have more words, and

Floyd punches Foley in the nose! The war is on again, but this time it doesn't stop with Floyd and Mr. Foley. News of the feud spreads, and before you know it, the whole town of Mayberry is involved. People are punching each other in the nose without even knowing why. The lines have been drawn. You are either in Floyd's camp or Foley's camp. There is no in-between. Even Opie and his young friend Johnny Paul get involved in the battle. Finally, Andy has had enough. He calls Floyd and Mr. Foley to the courthouse and is determined to work this out before any more damage is done.

After he gets rid of Barney, who started the whole ruckus in the first place, Andy has a serious discussion with Floyd and Mr. Foley. Obviously, the two have been acting like spoiled kids, but the issue goes much deeper than that. You see, Floyd and Mr. Foley have been friends and neighbors for years. They have helped each other and seen each other through a lot of hard times in the past. And here they are acting like enemies just because they had a disagreement about a quarter shave twenty years ago! Andy emphasizes the rarity and the value of old friends and reminds them of the first law of friendship, which in Andy's words is to be ready to forgive. When Floyd and Mr. Foley cool off and think about the situation, they both realize how ridiculous their behavior has been. Andy suggests that nothing has been done that a warm handshake won't fix. Floyd remembers Sheriff Poindexter told them the same thing twenty years ago. Andy asks, "If it worked then, why not give it a try now?" Floyd and Mr. Foley consider it for just a moment before enthusiastically shaking hands.

This story turned out well, but how many similar stories might not end so well because Andy is not there to remind us of that first law of friendship: forgiveness. When you stop and think about what causes us not to forgive each other, several things come to mind. Pride, stubbornness, selfishness, anger, and hurt feelings all can preoccupy us. Floyd and Mr. Foley were ready to end a lifetime of friendship, and for what? An argument about a quarter. We can laugh at the situation, but consider our lives and relationships. It is so easy for us to get all up in arms because we think our rights have been trampled—that we have been wronged. And we're not going to rest until our side of the story is heard. This kind of attitude destroys unity, and we can see by the example in the episode that the attitude is contagious. People were fighting each other without even knowing the real issue.

The case of Floyd and Mr. Foley can teach us two important lessons: how to deal with pride and how to put on humility. Both men were so concerned about their side of the story that they didn't care about anything else. They obviously didn't consider the silliness of the issue; but more importantly, they didn't care about the damage they were doing to each other and to the town. It's easy to get caught up in defending an issue, whether it is personal, professional, or even spiritual. We will always have differences of opinions with our families, at work, and at church. But what is the wisdom of defending a point to the detriment of everything else? Chances are, we will end up like the people in the town of Mayberry—everybody fighting but no one knowing why. Eventually, Floyd and Mr. Foley realized the seriousness of the issue and made amends. They realized that the preservation of their friendship was much more important than touting their side of the story. If we can learn Andy's first law of friendship—to be ready to forgive—maybe we can also put the concept of "our rights" in the proper perspective.

MAYBERRY AFTER MIDNIGHT

"Opie's Newspaper"

*Get rid of all bitterness, rage and anger, brawling and
slander, along with every form of malice. Be kind and
compassionate to one another, forgiving each other, just as
in Christ God forgave you.*

Ephesians 4:31–32

Have you ever noticed the number of verses in the Bible that
teach against gossip and slander? I have to admit, I was a little surprised after performing my own research on the subject. Usually when you think of sin, gossip doesn't come to
the forefront. Looking back on biblical examples of human
failures, we readily remember Cain for his brother's murder,
David for his adultery with Bathsheba, and Judas for his be-
trayal of Jesus. But how many people do we remember for
their slander and gossip? Chances are, not that many. So I
wonder why we are repeatedly warned about the evils of
such activity.

"Opie's Newspaper" is a story of how such gossip almost
blew the town of Mayberry wide open. Opie's friend, Howie,

received a small printing press as a gift, and the boys decide to go into the newspaper business. They work hard and produce an initial issue of the *Mayberry Sun*. The boys soon find that business is pretty slow, so they ask Andy and Barney for advice. It seems that the boys' newspaper is full of information about their class at school, but that's about it. Barney advises Opie that they need to widen their scope to attract more readers. Andy also encourages the boys but reminds them that the main thing to remember is to have fun with the project.

Opie and Howie decide to examine the real Mayberry paper to determine how they might improve their own publication. After reviewing sections such as "Washington Roundup" and "Social Security in Action," both boys realize that the adults are most interested in a section called "Mayberry after Midnight," the gossip column. Howie and Opie conclude that if they are going to be successful, their paper will have to contain similar information. So they put on their reporter hats and set out to gather as many "exclusive stories" as they can.

Fortunately (or unfortunately, depending on how you look at it), there is no shortage of such news in Mayberry. Opie overhears Aunt Bee talking on the phone about how Mrs. Foster's chicken-à-la-king tasted like wallpaper paste at a recent function. Howie hears Andy talk about how the town of Mayberry is lucky to have their preacher, but his sermons are as dry as dust. Barney and Aunt Bee unknowingly discuss the marriage of Harold and Sue Grigsby in Opie's presence. Aunt Bee claims that Harold is old enough to be Sue's father, and Barney notes that the only reason Sue married Harold is because he owns half of the local sawmill.

Furthermore, Barney states that the younger Sue is a blonde right out of a bottle. Opie and Howie collect all this information for their second edition of the *Mayberry Sun.*

Barney, Andy, and Aunt Bee are all in the Taylors' kitchen when Opie delivers the second issue of the paper. Opie leaves to continue his delivery, and at first no one notices anything wrong. They compliment the hard work and effort of the boys and how they are really trying their best. But just as he is getting ready to leave, Barney notices a headline, "Barney Fife says Sue Grigsby Blonde from a Bottle." Then it all breaks loose! The scramble is on to retrieve all the newspapers before it's too late.

I think the telling quote of the whole story is Opie's response to Andy when Andy scolds him for printing stories that are mean and unkind instead of stories that are nice. Opie responds by saying that when they included nice stories in the paper, no one wanted to buy it. When you fast-forward to today, think about what sells in our society. Is it the nice stories Andy is talking about or the more sensational tales? One look at the magazine rack at the local grocery store can answer that question. And what about us? Do we tend to encourage one another and build each other up, or do we take any chance to put each other down? It's just possible that we put others down in the hope that it will make us feel better about ourselves. Consider Aunt Bee. Maybe she was discounting Mrs. Foster as a cook because that was her territory. Maybe she thought Mrs. Foster presented some sort of competition to her own work. And what about the comments regarding the Grigsbys? Did it make Barney and Aunt Bee feel better by pointing out that the marriage was a bit unusual? Could jealousy have been a motive for their unkind words? Whatever the reasons, it is very difficult to build ourselves up by tearing others down.

The consequences of the gossip are not fully realized in the episode because Andy and the others involved are able to gather up all the newspapers before anyone has a chance to read what was printed. That is, except for the preacher. Andy is forced to endure a very embarrassing moment on the preacher's front porch because of the "dry as dust" comment. The irony in the situation is that Andy was actually in the process of giving the preacher a compliment when that particular comment slipped out. He was commenting on how lucky the town of Mayberry was to have a preacher such as this man, but the uplifting comment by Andy never made it to press.

When you think about gossip, it's easy to think that it's no big deal. Everybody does it, right? But when you really think about its consequences—hurt feelings, isolation, division, broken trust, and damaged relationships—the deal suddenly gets much bigger. All of these consequences can result from an ill-advised comment or divisive statement. With one slip of the tongue, relationships can be destroyed. Perhaps that is why we are warned over and over again about the dangers of gossip. In the end, Aunt Bee realized that they, as adults, were responsible for what happened with Opie's newspaper. She states that if they had been better examples to the boys, the whole situation would have never happened. Regardless, I believe Opie and Howie learned a valuable lesson on the dangers of "widening their scope" in the newspaper business. Hopefully we can learn a lesson as well, a lesson my mama tried to teach me a long time ago—if you can't say anything nice, don't say anything at all.

CHAPTER 26

WHAT, ME WORRY?

"The Lucky Letter"

"Peace I leave with you; my peace I give you. I do not give to you as the world gives. Do not let your hearts be troubled and do not be afraid."

John 14:27

OK, I have to admit it. Under this calm and collected demeanor, I am a high-stress individual, or should I say a high-stressed individual. It doesn't take much to peg my internal anxiety meter. The longer I live, however, the more I realize that the things I worry about are the very things I have no control over. Furthermore, a lot of things I spend my time fretting about never happen. It seems that some people naturally expect the best out of life, but the converse of that statement is also true. Some people do expect the worst, and if I am not careful, I can fall into that category.

Why do we worry and allow ourselves to get all stressed out? Is it our environment, a lack of faith, or are we just born that way? Furthermore, do we bring some of our troubles on ourselves? Barney was in a particular situation I can relate to. He allowed himself to get all worked up over something silly. At the time, however, the situation wasn't silly to Barney. The episode "The Lucky Letter" opens with Barney receiving a chain letter in the mail. Even though he discounts the effects a chain letter could have on his life, Barney immediately begins to type the two copies of the letter so as not to break the chain. Andy gives Barney a hard time about being superstitious, but Barney insists that he is just being "cautious." Andy persists, and finally a frustrated Barney drops the whole idea. He ends up throwing away his copy of the letter.

Then the trouble begins. Just like the letter warned, bad things start happening to Barney. He cuts himself shaving, he bumps his head, and a truck runs over his foot. Barney begins to think he is cursed. To make matters worse, Barney is supposed to participate in pistol qualifying, which is a yearly test required of all sheriffs' deputies. With his streak of bad luck, he begins to wonder if he will even keep his job. Andy tries to calm Barney by telling him that all of this is just a coincidence. Andy also reminds Barney of the dangers of thinking about all the bad things that can happen until they eventually do. Andy suggests that Barney try to forget about his troubles for a while. He tells Barney to call Thelma Lou and have a nice, quiet evening at home. Barney agrees and takes Andy's advice. However, when he calls Thelma Lou, he finds that she is busy. It seems that Thelma Lou has plans to spend the evening gluing covers back on hymnals at the church building with Edgar Coleman. Barney automatically assumes that something is amiss and gives Thelma Lou the ultimatum. It's either Barney Fife or Edgar Coleman, and that's about the situation as he sees it. Thelma Lou promptly hangs up on Barney.

In a span of just a few hours, Barney has lost his girl, his job is in jeopardy, and he is afraid to go outside because of what might happen to him. A fine state to be in for the pistol qualifying. Andy suggests that Barney brought a little of his trouble on himself, but Barney isn't listening. He believes that he is finished, that it is all over. He is defeated.

It's fun to laugh at the antics of our beloved deputy, but I wonder if I am that different from him. I may not get all

worked up over a chain letter, but plenty of things in my life can get me just as rattled. This episode causes me to reflect on how I handle the stress of everyday life. Of course, I know that struggles and challenges will happen, and I will have to deal with them. But am I guilty of needlessly bringing worry and stress on myself? In other words, am I the cause of my own stress because I'm worrying about something just for the sake of worrying? I am reminded of the first time I traveled to Germany on business. I was traveling with three coworkers to do some software demonstrations for an American military customer. Fortunately, the front end of the trip was not overly taxing, and we got to do quite a bit of sightseeing. My boss, who was a retired army colonel, showed us a great time in Munich, Rothenburg, and other picturesque cities of that beautiful country.

After a few days of play, we settled in to the business at hand. We were demonstrating some state-of-the-art simulation capabilities to several high-profile military officials. Basically, we had a series of computers set up in a briefing room. Mike, a coworker, and I were the computer experts, and the other two traveling companions, including my boss, were the marketers. During one presentation, we had several high-ranking officers in attendance and it was important for us to perform well. When we gave a presentation, the marketing guys would give a thirty to forty-five minute briefing; then Mike and I would do the actual computer demonstration.

The room was fairly large and full of officers interested in our technology. John and Brian were flipping view graphs and providing background information for the demonstration. Mike and I were at the computer consoles waiting for our part of the presentation. The room was full and it was getting quite warm.

During the briefing, I began to feel some tightness and pain in my chest. I didn't really worry about it at first. I just attributed it to nervousness and the fact that it was very warm in the room. But the longer the briefing went on, the more uncomfortable I began to feel. Finally, it was time for us to give the computer demonstration. Mike and I performed flawlessly, but the pain was getting much worse. I was concentrating more on not passing out than on the demonstration itself. After what seemed like an eternity, the demonstration was over. The room emptied and we went out into the lobby. It was cooler there and I began to feel better, but I was still concerned. Since we were on an American military base, I thought there might be a nurses' station I could visit to see if anything could be done. I casually asked one of the resident military guys if there was such a station, and he said there was, but at this hour it was probably already closed. He asked if there was anything he could do, and that's where I made my mistake. I quietly told the guy I was having some chest pains and was hoping the nurse could look me over.

The guy immediately thought I was dying. He screamed, "My goodness man, we've got to get you to a hospital; you might be having a heart attack!" Now, it might be helpful to know that at that time in my life I was somewhat of a hypochondriac. The mere mention of an illness could cause me to have symptoms. At that point I was indeed convinced I was a twenty-eight-year-old male having a heart attack on foreign soil. My next thought was that I had to get to a hospital, because I probably didn't have much time. I immediately found Brian and asked him if he could take me to the hospital. He looked at me like I was an idiot until I explained the symptoms and the fact that that military guy thought I was having a heart attack. Brian agreed that I should probably get checked, but neither of us had the faintest idea of where to find a hospital in the middle of Germany.

As rumor of my serious condition spread, we found out from one of the locals that there was an American military hospital just down the road. Brian and I got directions and left. While in the car, I gave the written directions to Brian in case I became unconscious during the trip. We got on the road and it became very quiet. All I could think about was that I was probably going to die, and they would have to ship my body back home like a fallen war hero. Poor Brian tried to cheer me up by telling me some story about a family member who had heart trouble, but to be honest, I don't remember anything he said. I just knew I was a goner.

We finally got to the hospital, and they hurriedly put me in an observation room. The attendants removed my shirt and my shoes and quickly placed monitors all over my chest. It must have been a slow night because there were at least a half dozen nurses there poking and prodding and taking different readings. A couple of doctors came in and asked me a few questions. Basically, they looked at me kind of quizzically, then left the room. The nurses began to finish what they were doing, and they began to leave as well. Eventually, I was alone in the room with a lot of beeping equipment around me. I could see the monitor above me, and it sounded like my heart was still beating at a fairly regular rate. I was feeling some better about my survival chances, but my chest still really hurt.

After several more minutes, one of the doctors came back in the room. He took one look at the monitor and said that from all indications I appeared to be one of his more healthy heart patients. I could tell by his expression that I was probably going to live. He sat down and asked me several questions, trying to pinpoint where the pain was coming from. After asking about my current physical status, he began to ask other questions, such as why I was here and what I had been doing when the pain started. It was becoming obvious that this pain was not associated with a stressed heart, but rather with a stressed individual. Even though I was not aware of it, I was under quite a bit of stress from the travel and the pressure to perform. The doctor and I talked a while longer, and then he released me to go back to the hotel.

Later that night, I realized how I let a little situation explode into a life-threatening crisis—in my mind anyway. I began to think of ways to handle not only the big stresses of life, but also the everyday stresses that can build up over time. I slowly realized that after I was told that nothing was wrong, the pain in my chest had slowly disappeared. When I got back to the States, I went ahead and had a full physical, just to be sure. All the results came back fine and I was given a clean bill of health. However, this event stuck in my mind. Until it happened, I never really believed that emotional stress could cause physical symptoms. But I realize now that it can happen very easily if I allow it to.

Sometimes I get so caught up in my profession and in the other activities of my life that I don't realize the stress I bring on myself. In this case, it took a sharp pain in the chest to make me realize that I wasn't handling things very well, even though I was not initially aware of any problems. When you stop and think about it, most of the things we get so worked up over don't really matter that much, but we needlessly bring the stress on ourselves anyway. Through my experience I learned an important lesson on stress management, but I also learned how to avoid letting things get to me in the first place. Now when I feel myself getting all worked up, I try to stop and take a little time to get myself together. Usually I reflect on the situation and try to put it in its proper perspective. I have begun to realize that whatever I worry about is really not all that bad. In fact, it's usually something I can handle quite easily. It just takes a little while to remember what's really important.

So, what happened with Barney's pistol qualifying? Unbeknownst to Barney, Andy had arranged for Thelma Lou to meet them at the firing range. When Barney realized that Thelma Lou still had faith in him, that's all it took. Her uplifting meant more to him than any chain letter, and his nervousness and stress immediately left him. Barney passed the qualification with a perfect score.

CHAPTER 27

LIFE SAVER MAN

"Andy Saves Gomer"

This is how God showed his love among us: He sent his one and only son into the world that we might live through him. This is love: not that we loved God, but that he loved us and sent his Son as an atoning sacrifice for our sins.

1 John 4:9–10

Andy stops by Wally's Filling Station one day and finds Gomer Pyle asleep on the job. Not only is Gomer asleep, but a fire is smoldering in one of the trash cans inside the filling station. Andy wakes Gomer and quickly puts out the fire. Gomer can't believe he was so careless and credits Andy with saving his life. In the coming days, Gomer feels completely indebted to Andy. He washes the squad car, mows the grass, cuts the firewood, and even catches fish for Andy. All of this attention is not limited to just Andy. While he is at it, Gomer tries to help out Opie and Aunt Bee as well. Gomer promises to always be by Andy's side in return for saving his own life.

While Andy appreciates Gomer's good intentions, all of this dedication starts getting to him. He can't go anywhere without Gomer tagging along asking if there is anything he

155

can do for the "Life Saver Man." Furthermore, Gomer em-
barrasses Andy by telling anyone who will listen about the
bravery and heroism of the town's sheriff. It gets so bad that
Andy, Opie, and Aunt Bee have supper one night in a jail cell
down at the courthouse, just to have some peace from
Gomer. Andy begins to realize that the only way things will
ever return to normal is if Gomer saves his life.

Andy devises a little plan. He rigs the gas furnace at the
courthouse to have a leak. Then he calls Gomer and asks
him if he will bring his jacket from home. The plan is that
Gomer will walk in, see Andy "passed out" by the gas furnace, and save the day. Unfortunately, the plan doesn't turn
out exactly the way Andy intended. Before Gomer arrives,

Opie walks in and finds Andy on the floor. In a funny scene, Andy explains his awkward position by pretending that he was actually doing push-ups. Opie tells Andy that he needs some help out back, and Andy rushes out to assist Opie before Gomer arrives. Meanwhile, Gomer enters the courthouse, smells the gas, and attempts to fix the leak with a wrench. Instead of turning the gas off, Gomer accidentally turns the valve wide open, and in the process, passes out from the fumes. Andy returns to find Gomer on the floor beside the furnace. He immediately turns the gas off and realizes that he has done it again. Instead of Gomer saving Andy's life, he has saved Gomer for the second time.

If you're familiar with *The Andy Griffith Show*, you know that it is impossible not to love the character of Gomer Pyle. His innocence, tender heart, and natural clumsiness just attract us to him. In the episode, "Andy Saves Gomer," we see yet another side of Gomer—his loyalty and devotion. Gomer is so appreciative to Andy for saving his life that he is willing to completely sacrifice himself to show his gratitude. As we can see, Gomer tends to take things to the extreme, but the point is still there. Gomer feels indebted to Andy for what he did, and he completely puts aside his own interests to show his gratefulness to Andy. For us, it's fun to watch the extent to which Gomer goes to show his appreciation to Andy. We even feel a little sorry for Andy because of Gomer's persistence. But I wonder if there is a lesson here as well. Andy kept playing down his part in saving Gomer, saying that the fire really wasn't that serious and that chances are, nothing would have happened. But that didn't deter Gomer. He really felt that Andy saved his life, and he was going to show his appreciation the only way he knew how.

In a very familiar verse to us all, we are told that God loved us so much that He sent His only Son so that we could have everlasting life. In effect, God made the arrangements to save our lives on a much grander scale, and all that is required of us is to have faith and accept the gift of salvation. But how grateful am I? Have I been exposed to the gospel for so long that I just take the gift of eternal life for granted? Or am I really appreciative for what God has done for me? Am I motivated to show Him my appreciation for saving my life? God has done so much for me, and all He asks in return is that I believe in Him and keep His commandments. Doing His will should not be a drudgery or something I have to do out of fear or obligation. It should be a response of love and appreciation. After all, He did make the supreme sacrifice to save my life.

CHAPTER 28

GOOD FOR WHAT AILS YOU

"Aunt Bee's Medicine Man"

"Come to me, all you who are weary and burdened, and I will give you rest. Take my yoke upon you and learn from me, for I am gentle and humble in heart, and you will find rest for your souls."

Matthew 11:28–29

It seems in this day and age that there is a remedy for everything that ails us. Whether we have a headache, stomachache, backache, or toothache, a specific pill or medicine is available to take care of it. It gets even more specialized than that. For example, the type of headache we have determines which medicine we should take. Is our headache attributed to allergies or stress or the flu? If you stop and think about it for too long, it can get rather confusing. Wouldn't it be nice to have one medicine for everything? No matter what our symptoms, we would know just what to take. If this were possible, there would be a lot less confusion at the local drug counter. Let's take it one step further. Wouldn't it be nice if there was one medicine that would take care of all our

problems, both physical and personal? Just one pill that
would cure everything. Now there's a pharmaceutical company I would want to buy stock in! Of course, it's silly to
speculate about such a wonder drug, but do we, in fact,
search for such a drug anyway? One that will take care of all
our ills? In the episode, "Aunt Bee's Medicine Man," Aunt
Bee is searching for something that will solve all her problems and give her a new lease on life. But does what she
finds really help her situation?

The episode begins with Aunt Bee arriving at the courthouse extremely distraught. It seems that an acquaintance,
Augusta Finch, has passed away. What makes this event sig-
nificant is that the late Augusta Finch was exactly the same
age as Aunt Bee. This news doesn't sit well with Aunt Bee at
all. She wanders into the courthouse, and Barney immediately notices that something is wrong. Moments later Andy
comes in and is also concerned. A stricken Aunt Bee describes what a blow this news is to her. Andy is a little confused because he doesn't remember Aunt Bee and Miss
Finch as being close. However, when Aunt Bee comments on
their similar ages, Andy begins to understand. The passing
of Augusta Finch has caused Aunt Bee to dwell on her own
mortality, and she doesn't want to admit that she is getting
older. When Andy suggests that a physical exam might set
her mind at ease, Aunt Bee angrily responds that all the doctor will do is tell her that she isn't a spring chicken anymore.

A little later, Opie calls Aunt Bee's attention to a peculiar
street vendor who just arrived in town. It seems that a man
named Colonel Harvey is selling a wonder medicine that will
cure whatever ails you. Colonel Harvey claims that at one
time in his colorful past he lived with the Indians, the

Shawnee to be exact. During this time he was made aware of a wonderful "Indian Elixir" that would cure anything from a common cold to depression. Colonel Harvey just happens to be selling this wonder drug for just a dollar a bottle. Aunt Bee can't believe what she is hearing. Maybe this is just what she needs. She immediately speaks up and buys two bottles. The enthusiasm spreads and everyone gathered around the truck begins buying bottles of the elixir.

When Andy and Barney arrive at the Taylor house that evening, they are in for quite a surprise. They walk in the front door to find Aunt Bee and Opie singing at the piano. Andy states that he can't remember the last time Aunt Bee played the piano like that. Furthermore, it seems that Aunt Bee is a little unstable. If Barney didn't know better, he would say she was "tiddly." Andy agrees but reminds Barney that Aunt Bee won't even allow a fruitcake in the house. However, when Barney looks in the closet to retrieve his raincoat, he notices a half-empty bottle of the colonel's elixir. Barney and Andy share a knowing look, and Andy instructs Barney to take the bottle and have the contents analyzed. Meanwhile, Andy finds out that Aunt Bee has invited none other than Colonel Harvey for dinner.

While Opie and Aunt Bee are completely taken by Colonel Harvey's presence, Andy is a little more skeptical. However, Colonel Harvey manages to avoid all of Andy's pointed questions about his history and the product he is selling. The evening ends with Colonel Harvey accepting Aunt Bee's invitation to speak at the Ladies Aid Church Committee the next day. The following morning Barney returns with the elixir analysis results. The stuff is actually 85 percent alcohol, thus explaining Aunt Bee's unusual behavior of the day before.

Barney wants to immediately arrest Colonel Harvey, but Andy decides to wait. He wants to expose Colonel Harvey for the phony that he is. Andy shows up at the ladies' committee meeting to find that the ladies are indeed gassed. However, Andy's statement that he is "raiding" the party, and that all the attendees are under arrest sobers the crowd very quickly. Andy transports the ladies to the courthouse and provides them coffee to assist in the recovery. Barney brings in Colonel Harvey, and the ladies, especially Aunt Bee, give the colonel a piece of their mind.

This episode reminds me of a song from my youth. Being a child of the eighties, one of my favorite music groups was Huey Lewis and the News. In 1983, one of their top songs was "I Want a New Drug." Now, I don't believe that Huey was promoting the use of illegal drugs with that song. In fact, Huey Lewis dedicated much of his public effort to encouraging kids to stay straight and make something of themselves. This particular song described his futile attempt to find a "new drug" that would solve all his problems, but without the side effects. It was a humorous song, but I don't think it was that far off the mark. It reminds me of my tendency to search for the quick fix instead of addressing the real problem. I think we can understand why Aunt Bee was feeling low. It happens to all of us at one time or another. Some event or occurrence will remind us that we are just mortal humans. Instead of facing her fears and uncertainties, Aunt Bee turned to a quick fix, a wonder drug that would solve all of her ailments and make her feel young again. Unfortunately, this "elixir" ended up doing more harm than good.

When I face problems in my life, it may seem easier to go for the quick solution, the solution that makes me feel better for the moment but ultimately doesn't do much to address the real issue at hand. It's much harder to be honest with myself and really examine the issues in my life that need some attention, because when I take that hard look at myself, sometimes I find things I just don't want to deal with. I would much rather apply a temporary fix than to take the time and make the effort to get to the root of the problem. But in my heart, I know that it is the right thing to do. It might not be the easiest approach, and it might not

involve the use of a magical elixir, but it will provide the lasting results I need.

Aunt Bee was ready to try anything to make herself feel better, and sometimes we may have the same attitude. But how often do we search in the wrong place for the cure?

Jesus promises us comfort if we will bring our struggles and heartaches to Him. He will heal us and make us whole again. In our fast-paced world of instant treatments, it's easy to forget that He has the miracle cure. It is the miracle of His life and death, and it's available just for the asking.

FATHER KNOWS BEST

"Bringing Up Opie"

My son, do not forget my teaching,
but keep my commands in your heart,
for they will prolong your life many years and bring you
  prosperity.
Let love and faithfulness never leave you;
bind them around your neck,
write them on the tablet of your heart.
Then you will win favor and a good name
in the sight of God and man.

Proverbs 3:1–4

Opie has it made. Not only does Opie live in Mayberry, but his dad is the sheriff, and that means he gets to stop by the courthouse every day after school. Compared to most boys his age, this must be a pretty big privilege. How many other kids actually get to pin up "Wanted" posters, or practice the quick draw with Deputy Fife. I bet that even emptying the trash at the courthouse seems important compared with doing chores at home. The best part, however, has to be listening to Andy. As most of us know, Andy really has a knack for telling a good story. Whether it's "Beauty and the Beast" or "King Arthur and the Knights of the Round Table," Andy can always hold your attention.

Yes, Opie pretty much has it made. That is, until Aunt Bee steps in. It seems Aunt Bee is unimpressed with some of the things Opie is picking up around the courthouse. Opie begins developing a vocabulary that is somewhat questionable for a boy of six or seven. For example, describing Otis as having "a snoot full" doesn't win many points with Aunt Bee. Opie is also disciplined at school for handcuffing a fellow student to a flagpole. One look at Barney, and it is pretty clear where Opie got the handcuffs in the first place. Considering all this, Aunt Bee decides that the courthouse is not a suitable environment for a young, impressionable boy like Opie. The afternoon visits would have to stop.

At first Andy tries to pretend that this policy is for Opie's own good. Andy, Barney, and even Otis agree that they are probably bad influences on the boy. Otis admits that he is the worst example, but Andy and Barney tell Otis that they all have a responsibility to Opie. Opie takes the news well enough, but he soon finds that he has a lot of time on his hands. He tries to keep busy after school by enjoying some of Aunt Bee's milk and cookies, and he evens tries his hand at planting vegetables. But it just isn't the same. Planting spinach is no substitute for "Jack and the Beanstalk."

Eventually Opie begins to venture out on his own. He innocently begins to kick a can down the road, and before he knows it, he is out in the country. Opie barely escapes disaster when he ventures too close to an old abandoned mine that almost caves in on him while he is standing near the entrance. Later, another kid offers Opie some apples for his "kick can," and Opie happily makes the swap. After eating one too many, a tired Opie crawls up in the bed of a pickup truck and falls asleep. Unbeknownst to Opie, the owner of the truck comes out of the store and drives away.

By this time, Andy and Aunt Bee are frantic. It is getting dark, and they have no idea where Opie could be. Finally Andy receives a call and finds out that his son is OK. When Opie gets back home, Andy and Aunt Bee scold him for running away. However, when they stop and think about the events of the day, they can't remember any other time when Opie has pulled this stunt. Then it dawns on Aunt Bee. The reason Opie got into trouble was because he was left to himself. He had no guidance. There was no one there to show him the way. Aunt Bee begins to reconsider the wisdom of banning Opie from the courthouse. Sure, there were still some things around the courthouse that might not be good for Opie, but she had completely discounted the positive influences, the most important of which was his father. Without thinking, Aunt Bee had removed Opie's father from his life. What could have been more detrimental than that? Fortunately, Opie's adventure away from home makes Aunt Bee realize how important it is for the boy to spend time with his father. And, with a few adjustments, Opie's visits to the courthouse are reinstated.

This episode is a vivid example of how quickly a son can get lost without the direction and influence of his dad. Unlike Mayberry, our society today focuses on careers, business success, and material wealth. With all the distractions, when do we have time for the children? Are they a priority, or are they just one in a number of things we have to manage on a daily basis? Andy didn't have the perfect environment in which to raise his son, but he made time for him. Even when he had to work, Andy wanted his boy around just so they could spend time together. It didn't matter what they were doing as long as they were together. By making this time, Andy was building the foundations of a relationship that would last a lifetime.

Most people don't get it. Why do you like to go to a racetrack and watch a bunch of cars go round and round in circles? Well, there's not an easy answer. I don't know why I like it; I just do. I started following NASCAR Winston Cup racing about six years ago. Since then, I've had the opportunity to go to several races in such locations as Daytona Beach, Bristol, and Talladega. Talladega, the fastest of the tracks, is truly a spectacle to behold. When forty-three cars pass you at speeds close to two hundred miles per hour, it is a sensation that you will never get from watching the race on television. I believe everyone should attend at least one Winston Cup race. After attending a race, you will either think it is the dumbest thing you have ever seen, or, as in my case, you will be hooked.

Mike and I went to the time trials at Talladega on Friday. They usually hold time trials a couple of days before the race to set the starting lineup. Mike and I had originally planned to camp at Talladega, another whole aspect to the NASCAR faithful, but we decided against it at the last minute. Since we weren't camping overnight, we were able to take Mike's little boy, Scott. Now, Scott is a fairly typical six-year-old boy. He is full of excitement, energy, and mischief, and not necessarily in that order. We left Huntsville at 7:00 A.M. to arrive at the track a couple of hours later. It wasn't ten minutes into the trip when Scott began asking, "Are we there yet?" After a quick breakfast, we continued on. Scott never seemed to be happy with the seating arrangement. We started off with Mike in the back, Scott in the front passenger seat, and me driving. Soon Scott wanted to be in the back with his dad. Then he wanted his dad to drive and for me to be in the back with him. Then he thought we all should be in the front. This went on for a while until Mike and I decided that we should be in the front and Scott would ride in the back.

After a while, we stopped at a convenience store to get some coffee. It was about 8:30 A.M. and Scott wanted ice cream. Mike and I saw no reason why Scott shouldn't have ice cream, so we got Scott some ice cream. About three minutes later, Scott had ice cream all over his face, his shirt, his pants, his hands, and the majority of the backseat. For some reason, Mike and I didn't see this coming. Mike cleaned him up the best he could with a plastic grocery bag (all that was available), and we continued on. We finally arrived at the track, and we all ate a brunch consisting of doughnuts and Sprite. At racing events such as these, there are souvenir trailers for every team and driver imaginable. Naturally, we had to see all of them. Understandably, Scott was very interested in the car sponsored by the Cartoon Network. After finding the trailer, Scott found it hard to see the merchandise from his vantage point. A very helpful retailer offered to let Scott enter the trailer and look around. Of course, Scott accepted and basically told the nice lady that he would take one of everything. At this point, Mike had to step in and alert Scott that he could only have two items, not the entire stock. Scott decided on a cap and a shirt, and we were on our way to watch the qualifying.

To a six-year-old, qualifying is probably about the most exciting thing in the world, that is, for about ten minutes. Unfortunately, qualifying and practice can last a few hours. We arrived at our seats at about 11:30 A.M. and as expected, Scott was rather impressed with the cars, the noise, and the expanse of the track until about 11:45 A.M. At that point he needed to go to the bathroom, wanted to run up and down the stairs, wanted to eat Skittles, wanted to know where "Dale Dalehardt" was, wanted to lie down, wanted to know when they were really going to race, and the list went on. Also, about every three seconds Scott had some comment or question for me ranging from, "Mr. Joey, there goes your favorite car" to "Mr. Joey, did you eat all the Whoppers?"

The practice and qualifying were over, and we made it back to our car. As we were fighting the traffic, I noticed something I hadn't noticed all day long. It was quiet. Nobody was saying anything. I looked back, and there was Scott, sound asleep. For the first time that day, he wasn't asking to go to the bathroom, or spilling ice cream, or screaming for our attention. The sight of him made me think that we could have left Scott at home with a baby-sitter and had a much more peaceful day. We wouldn't have had to worry about keeping his seat belt buckled or taking him to the bathroom or how many bags of potato chips he had eaten. We wouldn't have had to worry about him falling onto the racetrack or listening to his incessant questions. However, if we hadn't taken Scott, he would have missed spending time with his dad. Sure it would have been more convenient for Mike and me, but would it have been better for Scott?

Looking back on the episode, Andy and Aunt Bee were understandably worried about the influences Opie was

subjected to at the courthouse, but that wasn't the most important issue. Of more importance was the fact that Opie
was actually spending time with his dad. Sure Andy was
busy and didn't have time to give his undivided attention to
his son, but they were together. By spending time with
Andy, Opie was able to see his dad as an example. He was
able to learn. Aunt Bee was concerned about the bad habits
Opie was picking up, but she forgot about the good things,
like becoming a well-behaved and responsible young man.
And who better to teach these things to Opie than his dad.

CHAPTER 30
THE FINAL FRONTIER

"Opie and the Bully"

I can do everything through him who gives me strength.
Philippians 4:13

Opie has a problem. A bully named Sheldon is forcing Opie to give up his milk money every morning before school. If Opie refuses, Sheldon says he will pulverize him, knock his block off, give him the old one-two, and jump on him. Pretty serious consequences for a kid. Opie doesn't want to admit he is afraid of Sheldon, so he says nothing about the situation to Andy. Andy begins to suspect something is up when he notices that Opie is asking Aunt Bee and Barney for milk money as well. Barney investigates and finds out the truth. Barney wants to alert Sheldon's parents about the extortion, but Andy will have none of it. He knows that it will be better for Opie to handle this one himself.

While Andy and Opie are fishing one day, Andy decides to use the opportunity to talk to his son about courage. Andy talks of a time when a bully named Hodie Snitch tried to lay claim to Andy's secret fishing hole. Instead of backing down, Andy explains that he met Hodie's challenge and tore into him like a "windmill in a tornado." Andy's encouragement begins to give Opie faith that he can stand up to Sheldon. The next day Opie prepares to meet Sheldon, and right before the showdown, Opie reminds himself of the things Andy told him. Using his faith in Andy as his strength, Opie stands up to Sheldon and not only teaches the bully a lesson, but he gets all his money back as well. Opie rushes back to the courthouse where Andy and Barney are eagerly awaiting his return. Andy has never been more proud of Opie and the courage he displayed in standing up to the bully.

When I thought of courage as a kid, I thought of the astronauts. I was born in 1965, at the height of the space race, and from an early age that's all I cared about. One of my first memories as a child was watching the first moon landing on July 20, 1969. I was a little over four years old at the time, and I remember that we pulled out the hide-away bed in the den and watched the landing until early in the morning. I still remember Walter Cronkite announcing that Neil Armstrong had successfully set foot upon the moon. Looking back, that event more than any other might have been the spark that ignited my interest in space. I remember imagining what it must feel like to be strapped into a tiny capsule, then blasted into the vast unknown reaches of outer space. While I was sure the exhilaration must have been incredible, I was equally sure it must have been a very frightening experience. I could only imagine the raw courage and bravery that the early astronauts must have possessed. Those men were my heroes, and I wanted very much to join their ranks.

When I arrived on this planet, this country was just getting good at sending men away from the planet, into Earth's orbit, that is. Project Gemini was in full swing the year I was born, and the Apollo program was not far behind. When I was a kid, my mom would offer me a choice on my birthday. I could have a birthday party at home and invite a bunch of kids over, or I could forego the party and go to the Space and Rocket Center in Huntsville, Alabama. I always chose the Space Center over some silly party. So every year in October my family would make our annual trek to the Space Center. As I grew older, my interest in space did not diminish. Even though the "glory days" of the Apollo program and the moon missions ended in 1972, my fascination with space travel continued. I remember watching the first space shuttle launch early on the morning of April 12, 1981. When space shuttle *Challenger* exploded in 1986, I was watching the launch from my dorm room in college. After graduation I returned to the place where I spent so many birthdays— Huntsville, Alabama. And while living here, I have been fortunate enough to work on several challenging technical programs, including the International Space Station.

When asked, most people can name the first human to step foot on the moon, Neil Armstrong. The question of who was the second man to walk on the moon is a little more difficult, but a lot of people (over the age of thirty-five, that is) can tell you that the answer is Buzz Aldrin. On the historic *Apollo 11* mission, Neil and Buzz were the first of six American crews to land safely on the surface of the moon and return to earth. A seventh crew, commanded by astronaut Jim Lovell, would have been the third mission to land on the moon, but an explosion of an oxygen tank in the command module forced the crew to abandon the lunar mission and return to earth. This seemingly forgotten story was recently revived in a dramatic fashion by the blockbuster motion picture *Apollo 13*, which, by the way, was directed by Mayberry's own, Ron Howard.

While the names of the first two men on the moon are easily recognized, can you remember the third astronaut on the *Apollo 11* mission? The one astronaut who did not descend to the surface of the moon but remained in the command module in lunar orbit while Neil and Buzz walked on the moon. Some of you fellow space buffs know that the command module pilot for the *Apollo 11* mission was Michael Collins. The reason I mention Michael Collins is because, in addition to being a fine astronaut, he is also a gifted writer. Several astronauts have written books about their adventures, but few can relate their story with the words that make the reader feel as if he were really there. Collins was also very open when describing his own feelings about the mission. While I might have thought that the early astronauts were men of steel and not afraid to face any challenge given to them, Collins was blatantly honest about describing his concerns and fears as he prepared for his part in this historic mission.

> Apollo 11 was entirely different. We were our nation's envoys, we three, and it would be a national disgrace if we screwed up. We would be watched by the world, including the unfriendly parts of it, and we must not fail. There was pressure to plan, to study, to concentrate, to explore each nook and cranny of my mind for some fatal flaw, something overlooked, something ill conceived, something I was supposed to do which I simply could not. To make it worse, only those of us inside the program knew the opportunities we had to fail, the unknowns in the equation; the rest of the world seemed to think it was already a fait accompli, but before Columbia became the Gem of the Ocean, there were a hundred close decisions and a thousand critical switch actuations facing us. A broken probe, a cracked engine nozzle, an electrical short, a crew lapse of attention, a jillion other things—and we would never make it. I don't know about Neil and Buzz, because we never discussed these things, but I really felt this pressure, this awesome sense of responsibility weighing me down, this completely negative sensation, this commandment which said, Thou shalt not screw up.[1]

At the time of the mission, you would have never known that Collins had any of these concerns. You would have never doubted his self-confidence or faith that everything was going to work out fine. During the mission, he went about his job with the greatest of precision, and the flight of *Apollo 11* was an astounding success. But Michael Collins's personal reflections give us an indication of the human side of the story. Many unknowns faced the crew members. What they were doing had never been done before and sometimes all that was left was courage and faith—faith that all the hard work and dedication of those associated with the program would be realized, and the courage to face a daunting situation alone.

From the moon to Mayberry. Opie also faced a daunting situation. Although it was not flying to the moon and back, it did require faith and courage. At first Opie didn't want anyone to know he was afraid, and he tried his best to keep it a secret. But Andy was able to teach Opie that in itself, being afraid is nothing to be ashamed of. The problem comes when your fear causes you to cower and withdraw. I'm sure Opie was still very afraid of Sheldon when he faced the bully for the last time, but this time he wasn't alone. He carried the faith he had in Andy, and that gave him courage—courage to face the situation at hand. This lesson reminds me that it's OK to be afraid as long as my fears don't paralyze me. But to prevent this from happening, I need courage to face the challenges in my life. And similar to Opie's situation, that courage comes from the faith I have in my heavenly Father.

1. Michael Collins, *Carrying the Fire: An Astronaut's Journeys* (New York: Farrar, Straus and Giroux, 1974), 348–49.

EPILOGUE

I do not want you to be ignorant, brethren, concerning those who have fallen asleep, lest you sorrow as others who have no hope. For if we believe that Jesus died and rose again, even so God will bring with Him those who sleep in Jesus.

1 Thessalonians 4:13–14, NKJV

In so many episodes of *The Andy Griffith Show*, the viewer can't help but notice the special relationship between Sheriff Andy Taylor and his son, Opie. "Opie's Charity" showed us how Andy let his pride get in the way when dealing with his young son. Andy assumed Opie was hoarding his money to buy his girlfriend, Charlotte, a frivolous present, but he was quickly humbled when he found out that Opie had planned to buy Charlotte a coat because her mother didn't have the money for a new one. In "Opie and the Spoiled Kid" we see Andy making himself available to his son. Andy had time for Opie and did not regard his questions as foolish. He took the time to listen, and by doing so, established a relationship of trust. The episode "Mr. McBeevee" presents Andy with a challenging situation. Andy knows that Opie has an active imagination, but Opie insists that his friend, Mr. McBeevee, is not make-believe but real. This statement is complicated by the fact that Opie describes Mr. McBeevee as being able to walk around in the trees as well as having other fantastic

abilities. In a touching scene, Andy decides that he does indeed believe in Opie, regardless of how far-fetched his story seems.

The Andy Griffith Show was a fictional television series, but it presented some very believable relationships—relationships in which we, the viewers, could readily identify. The love, patience, and gentle instruction that Andy provided Opie are some of the same attributes my father and grandfathers endowed to me as a young boy. And for this heritage, I am forever grateful.

His hands were huge. That's the one physical characteristic I'll always remember about my dad's father. I remember being in awe of Papa when I was a kid. He was a big man. He seemed at least seven feet tall to me. In a match with Goliath, I would have picked Papa to win. His hands seemed so big and strong that they could swallow you up. Even so, Papa was never intimidating, even to a little kid. He had such a gentle nature.

I will always remember Papa working with his hands. He was truly a craftsman, always very particular and attentive to detail. He and my dad built the house I grew up in. Papa helped to finish most of the interior of our house. He and my grandmother would drive approximately fifty miles every morning to work on the house until it was finished. At my mother's request, he built the cabinets in the kitchen out of the wood from an old barn. Only Papa could do that. Papa took pride in himself and in what he did, and that pride always showed in his craftsmanship.

What I am most thankful for is that Papa and my grandmother raised my dad. While growing up, one thing I remember about my dad is that he never lost his temper. Now, I didn't say he never got mad, but he never lost control. I believe he got that level-headed nature from Papa. I remember one particular time when Papa took us fishing. When he put the fishing boat in the water, he would always let me start the boat and drive it over to the dock while he parked the truck. I remember being just a little excited, and when I turned the key in the ignition, I actually broke the key. Here I was, dead in the water, and Papa walks up to the dock. I yelled to him that the key broke, but he thought I meant that one of the keys had just gotten bent. He yelled back to use one of the other ignition keys on the ring. At that point I further explained that I had actually broken the key off in the ignition and it was stuck in there. I could see his face drop, but he didn't get mad or yell. He just sighed, "Oh, Joey." When I finally paddled the boat over to the dock, he still couldn't get the broken key out of the ignition. But, he figured out a way to use a small blade on his pocketknife to turn the ignition and we were on our way. Vintage Papa. He could always find a solution.

I am grateful that Papa instilled in his son the values and principles that are so important. As I get older, I realize that those are the same values my parents tried to instill in me, and I realize the role my grandparents played in that process. Papa is gone now, but one physical reminder I have of him are my own hands. You see, I inherited the same big hands he had. Just one glance at my hands reminds me of my heritage and how important it is to me.

And although the visual image is not as easy as looking down at my own hands, the mental image of another pair of hands is very powerful. Just one glance at his nail-scarred hands gives me the same feeling. I know from whose family I come, and I know to whom I belong. It is those hands that often remind me of my eternal heritage, and one day I know those hands will lead me home.

In loving memory of Henry Lee Fann

Heartfelt thanks

to TAGSRWC (*The Andy Griffith Show* Rerun Watchers Club).

The Andy Griffith Show Rerun Watchers Club was founded in 1979 by four students at Vanderbilt University. The club now has approximately 20,000 members and 1,150 chapters around the world. For more information, write TAGSRWC, 9 Music Square South, PMB 146, Nashville, Tennessee 37203-3286. Or you can find out more on the worldwide Web at www.tagsrwc.com.

In June of 1998, the Twickenham Church of Christ in Huntsville, Alabama, began hosting the "Finding the Way Back to Mayberry" class based on episodes of *The Andy Griffith Show*. Since that time, the material has been used by several churches and organizations across the country. For more information on the Mayberry Bible study concept, visit Joey Fann's website at www.barneyfife.com.